Discover
the Suffolk
Coast

Terry Palmer

HERITAGE
HOUSE

First published May 1976 by Stourdale Press as The Suffolk Coast.

Revised, extended, second edition published by Heritage House February 1992.

Third edition, revised, published April 1996.

ISBN.1.85215.0491

Typesetting by Accent Typographics,
5 Gainsoborough Close, Colchester, Essex CO1 2NF.
Printed by Colorcraft, Hong Kong.
Published by Heritage House (Publishers) Ltd, Lavandou, Steam Mill Rd, Bradfield, MANNINGTREE, CO11 2QT.
01255.870595.

Acknowledgements. Ian Angus, Orwell Park School; Lotty Barbour, Easton Farm Park; Mrs Sylvia Belle, Nacton; Charlotte Barbour, Easton Farm Park; Paul Dixon, National Trust; Roger Eves, Ipswich Airport; Tim Gitsham, Ganges Museum; Geoff Gosling, Woodbridge Tide Mill; David Jordan, East Anglia Transport Museum; Tracey Lockwood, Polly Mullett, Felixstowe Dock; Geoff King, Richard Mainwaring, Pin Mill; Lyndsay Lardner, Wellcome Institute, London; David Lee, Southwold; Jamie McMullan, Shotley Point Marina; Simon Middleditch, Leiston; Ian Munday, English Heritage; Mrs Doreen Rayner, Felixstowe Museum; RNLI, Poole; Savills, Ipswich; Philip Wayre, Otter Trust.

Suffolk Coastal Path. Much of the charm of the coast is now accessible along the Suffolk Coastal Path, a footway established by the county council from Felixstowe to Benacre, then on to Lowestoft. The path leads through a wide variety of landscapes and if you plan to walk it, allow at least three days. You'll certainly discover the Suffolk coast!

Cover Picture ; Southwold Harbour

CONTENTS

MAPS

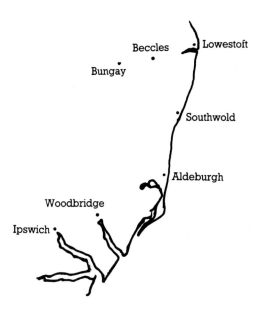

They used to weigh wool and corn at the Old Bell and Steelyard in Woodbridge

1: THE SUFFOLK COAST

Bird's-eye view

THE COAST OF SUFFOLK has been battling with the North Sea since the end of the Ice Ages, as the tides, setting from the north, tear away the soft cliffs of the north and deposit the rubbish by the rivers in the south of the county.

Look at the smooth coastline from Gorleston to Aldeburgh, then at the millions of tons of gravel forming **Orford Ness, and Beach**, and lesser amounts narrowing the Deben at Felixstowe Ferry, and at Landguard Point, Suffolk's southernmost tip. The **River Alde** once entered the sea at Aldeburgh and is even now only 100m from it, but the tides have built a gravel bank across the mouth forcing the Alde to travel another 10 miles (16km) before it escapes at Shingle Street. Even Landguard Point has grown several miles since the Norman Conquest.

Ipswich still has access to the sea, partly due to dredging, but the Waveney no longer takes small ships up to Beccles, as it did in Viking times.

Angle-land. The Vikings settled in Britain's northern isles and raided the east coast down to London, but it was the Angles from Angeln near Hamburg who settled the flatter lands, giving them the name **East Anglia** and the country Angle-land, ultimately **England**

The Angles divided into two groups, the *Nordfulk* and the *Sudfulk*, today's Norfolk and Suffolk, and they founded many settlements on an estuary, which they called a *vik*. Hence the North Estuary was Nordvik, or **Norwich**, and *Gipesvik*, the Gipping Estuary, became **Ipswich**.

Dunwich. There have been many changes over the centuries. The sea has swallowed all but the last trace of *Dunevik*, now **Dunwich**. **Iken** has risen and fallen; and the tiny hamlet named from Bishop Felix of Dunwich has become the largest container port in Britain - **Felixstowe. Lowestoft** was the leading port for trawler fishing but has now all but left that trade, and in recent years the hamlet of **Sizewell** has become home to two nuclear power stations, including Britain's last.

2: BETWEEN STOUR and ORWELL

The Shotley Peninsula

WHERE STOUR AND ORWELL meet is the best natural harbour between the Thames and the Humber – Harwich Harbour, holding a long-established ferry port, a newly-arrived container terminal, and a touch of Naval history.

Beyond the tidal limit the rivers themselves are tiny; their estuaries have made them important. The Stour's vast mudflats are a vital feeding-ground for birds while the Orwell has less mud and more marinas, and takes large ships under the Orwell Bridge to Ipswich Docks. But upstream of Ipswich it ceases altogether and becomes the Gipping.

The peninsula between the estuaries has no rail, no major road, yet has some surprising historical connections.

BRANTHAM

The Danes raided Brantham in 991, burning it to the ground and probably giving rise to its name of *brannt ham*, 'burnt village'. St Michael's Church owns Constable's painting of *Christ Blessing the Children*, but the work is now in safe keeping elsewhere. The village was home to one Thomas Tusser, the poet farmer who grew the first barley in East Anglia, and more recently to one of the world's first plastics factories – this one made Victorian shirt collars and table-tennis balls.

In 1994 the television comedy actor Melvyn Hayes became landlord of the Bull Inn, near the railway bridge.

STUTTON

The B1080 leads from the Bull Inn to Stutton, a long village with poor access to the river. But the church has some surprises.

St Peter's Church. Enter through the base of the 18m (60ft) tower and step into history, for most of the pews date from 1842 – look carefully and you can see that some had doors at their end. Woodcarver

Henry Ringham built most of them, as well as restoring 80 Suffolk churches, and he was one of seven carvers invited to submit samples for the rebuilding of the Houses of Parliament.

Parishioner John Page Reade didn't want Ringham's work and hung on to the family box pews, described as *huge, high, supported by Doric columns...and shabby for want of paint.* The pews were ripped out in 1880.

St Peter's had a barrel organ installed in 1832, for £70; when the congregation tired of the 12-tune repertoire, they bought another barrel.

Fairfax. In 1646 Thomas Fairfax was baptised here, a year after his father, William Lord Fairfax became Lord-General to Cromwell's army in the Civil Wars. Look closely in the cemetery for the headstone of Mary Sewell whose family paid £5 in 1789 to have her buried in a linen shroud. Why? Because the cottage-based wool industry of East Anglia was near collapse: the first large mill, near Bradford, was to open in 1798 and so help decimate the rural population of the eastern counties.

Alton Water. The reservoir which fills much of the valley of the Holbrook stream is a tourist attraction in its own right, with access from the B1080. Its capacity is 2,000,000,000 gallons or 0.216 cubic mile of water, destined for the Ipswich area, and Alton Hall and Tattingstone Hall are beneath its surface.

For more on Alton Water, see page 16

HOLBROOK

The picturesque 17th-cent **Holbrook Mill** stopped working in 1925 although its waterwheel had been removed in 1880 to make way for a turbine brought from Ontario. The mill was a restaurant in the early 1990s.

Royal Hospital School. Gifford Sherman Reade, a descendant of the Stutton man with the unpainted pews, was so impressed with the Royal Navy's achievements in World War I that in 1930 he left his 860-acre (348ha) estate to the Admiralty, with £1,000,000 to pay for the removal of the Royal Hospital School from Greenwich. Founded in 1712 for boys aged 11 to 18 who were sons or grandsons of naval officers, it had been financed by Greenwich Hospital.

It moved to Holbrook in 1933 to its new home in buildings named from famous naval commanders and is now a charitable trust. An Act of Parliament allowed the school to become co-ed in 1991 and abandoned the naval link for its 700 pupils.

Dardanelles cannon. The school's distinctive features are a 60.6m (199ft) tall tower visible for miles, and a cannon brought from the Dardanelles in 1804, with plaques marking eight naval victories from the *First of June* 1794 to 1840.

Anne Boleyn. Sir William de Tendryng, Lord of the Manor, decreed that he was to be buried *in* All Saints' Church; he also left £10 to build the north chapel. Sir William was great-grandfather to Sir John Howard who later became Duke of Norfolk and married Katharine Molyns in 1442: and this couple were grandparents of Anne Boleyn and of Catherine Howard, two of the queens of Henry VIII.

Church records hint that the nave had an earth floor until 1505 when Sir Richard Yngram willed 6s 8d (33p) towards the cost of paving.

You recall that Mary Sewell of Stutton was buried in a linen shroud in 1789? Bridget Greenleafe was buried in 1678 *in the churchyard...and she was not wrapt in any...shroud of any other material but sheep's wool, neither was the coffin lined with anything else.* One had to be seen to support the local industry, even in death.

Lower Holbrook. By the mill, turn east towards Harkstead and look for Lower Holbrook. At a sharp bend is a free car park by a path leading down to **Holbrook Bay** and a charming little harbour. A pity the water is contaminated by sewage.

The **Compasses Inn** has a timber from a barge as its fireplace lintel.

HARKSTEAD

Harkstead is a tiny village with a tiny church. Indeed, St Mary's is so small that the bellringers must stand around the font, in full view of the congregation.

ERWARTON

If Harkstead is small, Erwarton (sometimes spelled Arwarton) is minuscule, but St Mary's 13th-cent church held a treasure – the heart of Queen Anne Boleyn.

Read the wall plaque in the nave to start the story:

> Here lie the Remains of Sr Philip Parker, Baronet, and of Dame Mary, his Wife...He has represented the Borough of Harwich in three Parliaments...He is direct lineal heir male of Sr Henry Parker, KB, eldest son of Henry Parker, Lord Morley, by his second Wife Lady Elizabeth...Aunt to Queen Anna Bolleyn...1736.

Once again Anne Boleyn comes into the story. And she spelled her name as we do, as judged by this scale copy of her signature:

anne boleyn

Henry VIII. King Henry VIII had already divorced Catharine of Aragon and broken from the Church of Rome. In January 1533 he took his second wife, pregnant Anne Boleyn. The marriage was tumultuous, with Anne's anger frequently making Henry appear incompetent. When her child proved to be a girl, the future Elizabeth I, Henry was furious and soon took Jane Seymour as mistress. Anne's second baby was male, but stillborn.

Denied his male heir, Henry sent Anne to the Tower on 2 May 1536, charged with treason, adultery and incest. After the tribunal on 15 May Anne's five alleged lovers were executed, then on 19th May Anne herself was beheaded. Eleven days later Henry made Jane Seymour his third queen.

Anne's heart. Legend claims that Anne's heart was put in a heart-shaped casket and buried in Erwarton Church. Such a casket was found in the north wall in 1837, and when opened, contained dust. It's now in the vault below the organ.

If the story is true, why Erwarton? Because the Hall was then owned by Sir Philip Calthorpe whose wife Jane was Anne's aunt, and the Royal couple had visited **Erwarton Hall** several times. The place – not open to the public – was rebuilt in 1575 in brick, one of the first stately homes in this material. Its owner then? None but Sir Philip Parker.

East Coast barges preparing for the annual barge race

Back to the church for more of Sir Philip. This is the translation of the Latin inscription on his tomb:

> Here Philip Parker gravèd is in Place
> Of Philip Parker there is the onely Sonne
> And of his wife that Glemham's daughter was
> When he his race a yere [or] more had runne.
> Of Calthorpe, Baken and of D'Avyllier
> This impe as heir by lynage came,
> Three Antient Knights whose monuments are here.

There's another effigy: to Sir Bartholomew Daviller who died in 1287 after going on two crusades. At this time the Davillers owned the manor and three other estates, on condition that a family member lead the foot soldiers of Norfolk into Wales whenever it pleased the Royal fancy. For this service Daviller was to receive 4d (1½p) per man.

The Bacon family followed, its last female marrying Sir Oliver Calthorpe (see Calthorpe village in *Discover North Norfolk*) of Burnham Thorpe around 1400, explaining the last line in the poem. The Calthorpes gave way to the Parkers – which is where we came in.

Fairfax. Around the time that Fairfax was baptising his son at Stutton, he was laying siege to Erwarton. When the villagers ran out of shot they melted down five of St Mary's bells – there's still only one left.

Plague. Finally, look at the cross-shaped headstone to Mrs Gertrude Garrod who died 19 June 1918, one of several victims of the last outbreak of bubonic plague in Britain, although a lab worker died in 1962. The disease was first noted at Shotley in December 1906 and probably came on grain ships from San Fransisco, Valparaiso or Alexandria, all of which had plague at the time. It soon spread to Woodbridge, Hollesley and East Bergholt, with only six of the 22 victims surviving. Mrs Garrod, 42, of Warren Lane Cottages, fell ill on 16 June and was spitting blood on the 18th.

SHOTLEY
H.M.S. *GANGES*.

Shotley is famous for that mast, standing on the top of Bristol Hill and visible for miles. The original H.M.S. *Ganges* was a ship of the line which anchored off Falmouth in 1866 to train boy seamen. In 1899 it moved to Harwich then in 1903 to Shotley. But when the Royal Naval Training Establishment opened in 1905, the boys marched up the hill and *Ganges* sailed away.

The new 'stone frigate' needed a mast, so it used part of the foremast of H.M.S. *Cordelia* topped with sections of the mizzen mast of H.M.S. *Agincourt*. Total weight, 42 tons; height 43m (142ft), plus the 6m (18ft) buried in concrete.

The mast was needed to train boys in sailing techniques, but maybe it was an anachronism as steam had been used for 60 years. It was abandoned in 1914 and thereafter used for character-building and ceremony until the last mast-manning on 15 May 1973 when 82 boys climbed the rigging and Alan Ferguson was button boy, right at the top. *Ganges* closed in 1976.

The site owners and the *Ganges* Association restored the mast in 1988, but the ratlines are no longer load-bearing.

Police. The Home Office now leases the site for a college, training 160 police cadets from six counties for 15 weeks.

See Ganges Museum on page 17.

SHOTLEY MARINA

Bloody Point. Turn left at the Bristol Arms and you come to Shotley Marina, at the headland known locally as Bloody Point, near where Guthrum, the Danish king of East Anglia, was defeated by Alfred the Great in 885, the first recorded naval battle in British waters. In 1911 a special hangar was built at the point, from which a Commander Sampson tested a seaplane in Harwich Harbour. He was also the first man to fly a plane from the deck of a ship.

For more details on the marina, see page 32.

Shotley Church. Children of bygone generations used to chant:

> *Shotley Church without a steeple,*
> *Drunken parson, wicked people!*

The first line is true; the 15th-cent St Mary's hasn't a tower either, but it has a good hammerbeam roof. Nearby is a naval cemetery with 114 headstones from World War Two, mostly *Ganges* seamen but with a few Dutch and German sailors.

While you're here, look for the Victorian wall-mounted post box.

CHELMONDISTON

On 10 December 1944 a *Vergeltungswaffe Eins*, better known as a flying bomb or Doodle Bug, crashed on Chelmondiston, destroying the church and a nearby house.

The foundation stone of the replacement church was laid on 31 August 1955 and the resurrected St Andrew's was consecrated 18 months later. At first glance you'd swear it was the original, with its 14th-cent tower – but the old church had become so dilapidated by 1864 that it was declared unsafe and was mostly rebuilt in 1866.

Princess Muna. King Hussein, whose Kingdom of Jordan was

The Butt and Oyster pub at Pin Mill can serve drinks to people in boats

created by the British, took as one of his first wives one Princess Muna. She began life as an ordinary Chelmondiston girl who became involved with Arab high intrigue.

PIN MILL

Pin Mill is a tiny hamlet in Chelmondiston parish, but is famous for its boating links. The name may come from *pynd*, an old word for 'pond', and there was a mill and millpond some way up the hill. The hamlet also had several pans or ponds' for producing sea-salt.

But barges were the lifeblood of Pin Mill for generations. As Ipswich grew, and the size of ships grew, more seaborne traffic had to moor at Pin Mill to have its cargo offloaded into barges. This gave plenty of local employment, and even greater scope for smuggling; at the boom, three inns lived off the legal, and illegal trade, but the dredging of the Orwell in 1840 ended it all. The Riga Inn was the first to go, then the Alma, with only the Butt and Oyster surviving.

Arthur Ransome. Children's writer Arthur Ransome, best known for his *Swallows and Amazons*, set several books in East Anglia, with *We Didn't Mean To Go To Sea* beginning aboard a yacht moored at Pin Mill. Ransome (1884-1967) had his own boats built here at Harry King's yard, his *Selina King* being named from Harry's sister-in-law. Grandson Geoff now runs the family business.

There are barges everywhere at Pin Mill, some ready to sail in the annual barge race, some being restored, others aground and serving as houseboats, and too many rotting away into the mud.

The Butt and Oyster. The Butt and Oyster is one of the best-known pubs in Suffolk, not only for the Ransome link – there's a copy of *We Didn't Mean To Go To Sea* in the bar – but also because of its riverfront location. At high spring tide you can serve drinks direct to people in their boats, but during the East Coast Floods in the winter of 1952-53 the river came into the bar and put it under a metre of water.

The pub has a long association with bargees; in the old days the skippers would drink in the smoke room while their mates drank in the public bar. We don't know where Edward Seager drank, but his portrait of the inn is in the main bar.

The name? The oyster link is obvious, but pollution has killed them. Was the butt the barrel in which the oysters were sold, or was it the nearby archery butt?

Parking. Adequate space by the Butt and Oyster; other parking midway up the hill. *Don't park on the foreshore on the flood tide!*

National Trust woods. The National Trust owns the 85-acre (34ha) Cliff Plantation and Darwin's Covert woods east of the hamlet, with footpath access. At Cliff Plantation's eastern end stands Clamp House, the home of Konni Ziliacus, controversial Labour MP for Gorton, Manchester, elected in 1955.

WOOLVERSTONE

Woolverstone is such a small village that it has no shop, no post office, no pub, and the church is usually locked.

Woolverstone Marina. But it has a marina, with 200 deepwater berths at jetties and 146 swinging moorings; 01473.780206 for details. Ashore there are fuel, toilets, chandlers, and the Schooner bar-restaurant.

Cat House. Within the marina are the **Royal Harwich Yacht Club,** founded in 1843, and the privately-owned Cat House, built in 1793. When smuggling was rife, before the 1840 dredging, the owner of the house would put a stuffed or china cat in the riverside window, or a light at night, to indicate there were no customs officers around. The modern owner keeps a cat there all the time.

Wulf's Stone? An Anglo-Saxon village once stood here, and suffered from Viking raids. But was one raider named Wulf, and did he kill a villager on a stone brought down by the Ice Ages? Certainly in 1291 Hamon de Wolfreston was granted use of the land – and his name may have passed to the next village, Freston. But a later Lord of the Manor was Sir John Holbrook, whose grand-daughter left the estates to the Woolverstone family, who held them until 1580.

Next came the gentleman pirate Sir Thomas Gawdy, followed by the Cateleys, Bakens and Bedingfields, then John Tyson who went broke, John Ward, and William Berners who bought the lands in 1773 for £14,000.

Woolverstone Hall. Berners built Woolverstone Hall in 1776; he already owned Berners St, near London's Oxford St and Berners St in Ipswich. Geoffrey Berners sold the estate in 1937 to Lord Nuffield, who gave it to Oxford University – but remember the name: Berners.

During the war the Royal Artillery trained here and the Navy practised the Normandy Landings. In 1946 London County Council brought the London Nautical School, which became Woolverstone Hall School in 1959, when Oxford University sold out. Finally, Ipswich High School for Girls bought the hall in 1990, adding a sports hall and junior wing.

FRESTON

You need to be across the river for the best sight of **Freston Tower,** hiding in the woods of Freston Park. The folly is a tower of six rooms atop each other – but was it the work of Ipswich merchant Thomas Gooding in the 16th cent? Or was it for Ellen, heiress of the de Freston estate, so she could practise her six hobbies each in a separate room yet each with a river view? The tower is not open to the public, so you'll never know.

Woolverstone Marina, looking upriver to the Orwell Bridge

The restored Tattingstone Wonder still looks like a church from the front

TATTINGSTONE

If Freston Tower is a folly, then so is the **Tattingstone Wonder**. Squire Edward White built the Wonder around 1750 as three cottages for his workers, but arranged it so that it looked like a church when viewed from his home, Tattingstone Place. Two theories abound: he wanted to see a church; or that people would wonder about anything, so he'd give them something special. The Wonder has recently been restored as one house.

The **Church of St Mary** is unusual in that the entrance is through the *north* door, normally reserved for the Devil. The hammerbeam roof is good.

The village had two pubs until 1991, both unusual. Waterloo House was opposite the church, one of the smallest in the country (the smallest is in Cerne Abbas, Dorset) and in a wooden shed. It closed when rot was too rampant.

The other is the **White Horse,** across the causeway over Alton Water. The white stallion over the door once decorated the White Horse Inn in Ipswich but its masculinity offended the Victorians. The entire animal is now 'listed' for preservation, as is the nearby village pump. Strange, but the innkeeper who departed this life in the 1980s is said to come back to keep an eye on the pub. Maybe he's listed, too.

AND ELSEWHERE

Tiny **Wherstead**, overshadowed by the new Ipswich bypass has no shops, no pub, no post office, and the church is locked because two of its bells were stolen in the 1950s, on separate occasions.

Oldest house? Somewhat off the beaten track is **Little Wenham Hall**, notable only because it's claimed to be England's oldest brick-built house, with parts dating from the 12th cent. It's open on rare and random occasions.

Capel St Mary. The church of St Mary, Virgin and Mother has a rare **weeping chancel**, a kink to the right between nave and chancel when viewed from the west. This is said to signify Christ's head leaning to the right as he died on the cross, but it usually means another building was in the way and a kink was inevitable. A kink to the left is said to be evil, *sinister*.

●

ALTON WATER

The 400-acre (160ha) Alton Water offers an exciting range of activities in one of the most pleasant settings in Suffolk. Managed by Anglian Water, it lies in a secluded valley and if you enjoy walking, cycling, sailing, fishing, birdwatching, or a quiet picnic – it's for you.

At the main car park by the Stutton entrance you'll find a café and information point, and Alton Water Cycle Hire with a range of machines for all the family.

You may cycle or walk the eight-mile route around the reservoir, using a combination of surfaced and grass tracks, short sections of minor road, and the dam itself. Stop where you like for a rest, a picnic, or to watch events unfold.

The popular Alton Watersports Centre offers a range of courses for beginners to sailing and windsurfing, or you may launch your own dinghy or sailboard for a moderate fee. Annual membership is available, with boat parking at the waterside and nearby chandlery and catering.

The reservoir is known for its huge shoals of bream and pike, which make it popular with anglers. Day and season permits are available from the Cycle Hire shop, which also stocks a range of fishing tackle. Catches of more than 60lb (27kg) of bream have been taken in three successive seasons, which extend from 25 May to 14 March.

Call 01473.328873 for cycles, 327398 for fishing information.

Picture shows windsurfers.

See also page 7.

Hintlesham. Archbishop Stigand held the Manor of Hintlesham during Edward the Confessor's reign (1042-'66) and in 1052 was ordained Archbishop of Canterbury, says a record in **St Nicholas's Church** – but St Ethelbert's Church in Falkenham (chapter 5) lists all archbishops from 597 to 1903, omitting Stigand. Stigand certainly crowned Harold a few weeks before the Battle of Hastings, and he was later imprisoned in Winchester, where he died.

●

H.M.S. *GANGES* MUSEUM

One of the most famous of Royal Naval establishments is the celebrated H.M.S. *Ganges* at Shotley. Through its wrought-iron gates, from 1905 to 1976, entered thousands of lads, to exit as young men, having received the training that in two world wars, and in numerous conflicts all over the globe before and since, had equipped them to serve their country with valour and distinction.

Some little while after the closure in 1976 the H.M.S. *Ganges* Association was formed. It worked with the new owners, Potton Ltd, to preserve some of the buildings and especially the famous mast.

But the association's main achievement is the creation of the Ganges Museum in the Shotley Marina, with the marina owners' co-operation. The museum displays artifacts, memorabilia and photographs of the days of the Royal Naval Training Establishment, and is continually on the search for further exhibits. Obviously it cannot display the mast, nor the $2^{1}/2$ ton Indian Prince figurehead from H.M.S. *Ganges*, which is now at the Royal Hospital School, Holbrook.

The museum is open bank hols and weekends, Apr-Oct, donation welcome; for brochure or visits other times, contact (with s.a.e.): Museum Secretary, Mr G W Athroll, 20 Flint Close, IPSWICH, IP2 8PU; 01473.684740.

Picture shows the *Ganges* mast.

See also page 11.

●

Hintlesham's church is recorded in Domesday, 1086, and its first known rector was installed in 1160. But the drama surrounds the Timperley family. Sir Thomas, grandson of the third Duke of Norfolk, was the 16th-cent Lord of the Manor who built Hintlesham Hall. His son Nicholas refused to renounce the Church of Rome and was therefore stripped of all his assets.

Michael Timperley and his wife Frances, née Bedingfield, were also charged with Papacy in 1639 and fled to France where, true to their faith, they founded the Convent of Faubourg St Antoine which was to become a fashionable school in the 18th cent.

And finally, **William Dowsing**, the church desecrator, called in 1643 and broke 51 'superstitious pictures' – stained glass windows. But the brasses were stolen in the 19th cent Gothic revival.

Hintlesham Hall. Thomas Timperley's masterpiece was Hintlesham Hall, built in the 1570s and soon forfeited. In the 1720s Richard Powys, principal Clerk to the Treasury, added the Georgian front. **Robert Carrier**, the chef with the international reputation, converted the hall to a restaurant, while its more recent occupants made it into a 33-bed hotel. Guests can see the 17th-cent oak stair, walk the 175 acres (70ha) and try the 18-hole golf course.

The Orwell Bridge, looking eastward

3: THE ORWELL BRIDGE

And George Orwell

THE ORWELL BRIDGE had the longest pre-stressed concrete span of any British bridge when it was completed in December 1982. The centre span is 190m (623ft) long, almost the width of the river at that point.

Three years' work had gone into the building of the toll-free bridge, following debates on whether a tunnel would be better. The problem was that the bridge had to give headroom to ships using Ipswich docks at *high* tide, so the central span now offers 39m (128ft) clearance. But a tall bridge can be hazardous to motorists in high winds, so there are parapet walls as windbreaks – but they also spoil the view for car drivers.

The steeply-sloping ground on both banks meant that the bridge's approach roads started from sufficient height to avoid steep gradients or long ramps.

Despite the 100,000 cu metres of concrete which went into the structure, the Orwell Bridge can also be called a work of art. But art with a dual role, for inside the concrete box girders are power cables, telephone lines, and a 70cm (28in) water main from Alton Reservoir.

The contractors drilled 70 boreholes to test the chalky subsoil, then built 19 sets of piers, those holding the centre span rising almost 45m (150ft) from the bottom of their bases, deep underground. And the overall length? It's 4,218ft or 1.28km.

George Orwell. The novelist George Orwell has few local connections. Born in Bengal in 1903 as Eric Blair, he was educated at Eastbourne and Eton, died in 1950, and is buried at Sutton Courtenay, Oxfordshire. His best-known books are the political satires *Animal Farm* and *1984*.

4: IPSWICH

Wolsey and Dickens

NOBODY KNOWS how old Ipswich is, although the name suggests Viking links – *Gippes vik* being 'estuary of the Gipping'. The Romans bridged the Gipping to the north and forded the Orwell to the south, leaving the Anglo-Saxons to build the first settlement where the modern town now stands; most work was done between 850 and 1066, when the population was around 1,500 – a part of the Saxon ditch was found in 1975.

The Normans occupied the town, probably taking it intact. Domesday described it as `poor' but the Normans built a castle – destroyed in the 12th cent – and improved the earth dyke defences. Modern roads mark the sites with such names as Tower Ramparts, Westgate, and Northgate.

Maritime interests. The town developed its links with the sea, a tax return of 1282 showing that one person in eight owned a boat of some sort. King John had given the first charter in 1200, presenting it in St Mary-le-Tower.

Wool. Under Edward III (1327-1377), Ipswich became one of several east coast ports to benefit from the wool trade, which was England's basic industry for generations and gave East Anglia great wealth. In 1338, with the outbreak of the **Hundred Years' War** to protect our cloth trade, Parliament gave Edward half the wool in the kingdom – and he sold it to Flanders. He acquired wool by other means and used much of the proceeds to repay a loan of £2,500 on his queen, Philippa of Hainault. He even fleeced Ipswich customs to repay another loan from Florentine moneylenders. Despite that, the trade grew and in 1358 England exported some 13,000 sacks of wool and around 14,000 pieces of cloth; by the century's end the cloth trade outpaced the wool trade by 200 items to one.

In 1524 Ipswich was the seventh richest town in England and later, many of the refugee Huguenots entered England through here and Harwich.

King John's charter decreed that Ipswich be governed by a council of twelve men, originally merchants who were called Port Men. Read this inscription on the almshouses in Foundation Street:

Henry Tooley portman of Ipswich by his will dated Nov 15 1550 left several estates for the purpose of erecting Almshouses and for the maintenance of poor persons therein.

Tooley was unusual in opening up trade with Iceland, and his almshouses were rebuilt in 1846, the date of the plaque.

Portman Road. As the Port Men were unpaid they were granted grazing rights on a meadow, eventually being given the land, to be known as Portman's Marshes. The land was mortgaged in 1588 to finance two ships sent against the Spanish Armada, and over the years its name changed to Portman Road. Part of the marshes is now the ground for Ipswich Town Football Club.

CARDINAL WOLSEY

Thomas Wolsey, Ipswich's most famous son, was not a nice character. Born sometime between March 1471 and summer 1475 he was, according to Shakespeare, *fashioned to much honour from the cradle*, an easy assessment in retrospect. There was some truth in it, for he graduated with a BA degree from Magdalene College, Oxford, at 15, give or take four years, then became master of the prep school there. His architectural interests prompted him to build a tower for the college chapel, then he had to learn how to raise the money to pay

Ipswich's Customs House is dwarfed by Paul's granary

Marquis of Dorset. He got himself a patron, the Marquis of Dorset, before trying any more building – but as soon as he was rector of Lymington he modernised the church and rectory to excess, so that the Archbishop of Canterbury heard of it. When the marquis died, Wolsey was recommended to Henry VII as chaplain to the throne. In 1509 he became almoner to the new Henry VIII, who soon gave Wolsey a mansion as reward. Already Wolsey was ingratiating himself as the power behind the throne and, when Henry wanted to enjoy life and his new queen Catherine of Aragon, Wolsey took over some of the affairs of state.

Soon, anybody who wanted an audience with the king, had to bribe his way past Wolsey. But Ipswich's son was only just beginning. He contrived to be appointed the new Bishop of Ipswich, then he became Archbishop of York. A year later Pope Leo X made Wolsey a Cardinal.

Proxy king. It was a phenominal rise, from a relative nobody in Ipswich, and Wolsey cashed in. When the King of France wanted a treaty with England, he had to grant Cardinal Wolsey £12,000. The Holy Roman Emperor, the Duke of Milan, and even the Pope, found it prudent to grease his palm. In addition, Wolsey seized the incomes of the bishoprics of Hereford and Worcester, and bribes too numerous to mention.

He spent his fortune almost as quickly as he gained it. He had 800 household staff including 143 chaplains, and he demanded more pomp than the king himself. Entering Westminster Hall he had *two great crosses of silver borne before him, and his pursuivant-at-arms with a great mace of silver gilt*, wrote a 19th-cent historian. Even Wolsey's shoes *cost many a thousand pounds.*

Pope? Wolsey now had ambitions to become Pope, but the present incumbent, Adrian VI, was younger and fitter. But Adrian died mysteriously just 18 months into office. Wolsey never got the job: it went to Cardinal de Medici who became Clement VII.

Troubles. Wolsey was soon in trouble at home, for Henry tried to bribe this new Pope to allow him to divorce Catherine and marry Anne Boleyn. Clement refused, and so England broke away from the Catholic Church.

Wolsey retained his authority for a while and the next time he summoned Parliament was to levy a wealth-and-income tax of one sixth of people's assets (his own being exempt?). The plan failed, but Henry later used it as the excuse to destroy the nation's monasteries.

Hampton Court. Wolsey established a school in Ipswich and in 1528 began planning a college, but his control on the affairs of state was being wrenched away. He was obliged to give Hampton Court to Henry, but he was nonetheless thrown from office – and at 8am on 28 November 1530, the date and time he had prophesied some while

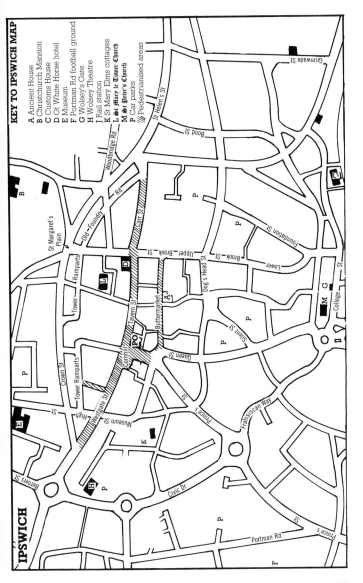

IPSWICH

KEY TO IPSWICH MAP

A Ancient House
B Christchurch Mansion
C Customs House
D Gt White Horse hotel
E Museum
F Portman Rd football ground
G Wolsey's Gate
H Wolsey Theatre
J Rail station
K St Mary Elms cottages
L St Mary le Tower Church
M St Peter's Church
P Car parks
/// Pedestrianised areas

Christchurch Mansion, Ipswich, was threatened with demolition in 1892

earlier, he died, in Leicester Abbey, where he was buried.

Wolsey's Gate. With him died Ipswich's school and the plans for the college, all that remains being a red-brick gateway leaning outwards in College St, north of the docks.

CHRISTCHURCH MANSION

In the 12th and 13th cents the Holy Rood Fair was held on St Margaret's Green, just outside the town walls on land owned by the Holy Trinity Priory, also known as Christchurch. After the dissolution of the monasteries the rights to the fair soon passed to the Withypool family. The fair sold cheese and butter every September, and was last held in 1844.

Edmund Withypool began building an elegant Tudor house on the priory site in 1548, calling it Christchurch Mansion. The Withypools grew so powerful that in 1628 Sir William marched out with his private regiment for a mass duel on **Martlesham Bridge**, where he shot the enemy leaders under a flag of truce. He was soon mortgaging the estate to pay the resultant fines, and bribe himself out of a prison sentence.

His daughter married Lester Devereaux, 6th Viscount Hereford, who made major alterations to Christchurch Mansion. Devereux was a member of Cromwell's Commonwealth government, yet he was also one of the six peers who invited Charles II to retake the throne in 1660.

24

The Devereux family sold to Claude Fonnereau in 1735, then in 1892 estate developers wanted to demolish the mansion. Felix Cobbold, banker and brewer, bought it for the Corporation and today Christchurch Mansion is the town's major museum, open daily, free, with Christchurch Park also open daily.

Museum. The mansion contains splendid examples of furniture and tapestries, and has a superb collection of household and kitchen tools of bygone ages. The **Wolsey Art Gallery** and the **Room Upstairs** are extensions of the museum.

IPSWICH MUSEUM

The town's only other major museum opened in 1847 in what is now Museum St, but moved to High St in 1881. The **natural history** section had the first gorillas to be seen in Britain, but it specialises in local wild plants. The other sections, geology, ethnology, archaeology and local history also confine their interests to south-east Suffolk. Open Mon-Sat.

Seeing the sights. The streets and houses of Ipswich are a museum in themselves, but you must search for the best examples. The **Tudor houses** where Cardinal Wolsey was born are on the corner of St Nicholas and Silent streets, with others in Oak Lane. The oldest inhabited houses, dating from 1467, are near St Mary Elms Church in Museum St, and the nearby **Black Horse** pub is probably the town's oldest.

The town centre, **Cornhill**, was a market place for 1.000 years, and nine people were burned alive here in the 16th cent for witchcraft and recanting their religion. St Mildred's Church, shown on the town seal of 1200, was the first Guildhall.

On Lady Lane, near the new Wolsey Theatre, a plaque marks the site of the **Chapel of our Lady of Grace**, which was the focus of medieval pilgrimages. The **Butter Market** was just that until 1810. Here is the **Ancient House,** built in the 15th cent, with superb plasterwork added in the 17th cent. North on Tavern St is the **Great White Horse Hotel** which is in records of 1571. It had a facelift around 1815 when the street was widened and its trademark, a rampant white stallion, was moved to Tattingstone White Horse for being too sexually explicit. **Charles Dickens** stayed here when he was working on the *Ipswich Chronicle* and reporting on elections, and he featured the hotel in *Pickwick Papers*.

North again is **St Mary le Tower Church** where you can attend lunch-time organ recitals on Tuesdays, May-Sep. A Sancta Maria ad Turrim church was here in Domesday times, the tower being part of the Saxon defences, as Tower St and Tower Ramparts are nearby. Later, the Merchant Guild of Corpus Christi was founded here.

Under the Commonwealth of 1649-60 the Town Lecturer was obliged to give a thrice-weekly sermon lasting 3 hours 30 minutes – the brother of an earlier lecturer had gone to Agawam, Massachusetts, in 1634 and renamed it Ipswich.

By St Margaret's Green is the town's other functioning Anglican church, **St Margaret's**, named from the queen of Malcolm III, King of Scotland; she died in 1090 and was canonised in 1250. In the churchyard lie the bodies of 440 victims of the **Great Plague** of 1665-66.

Move south, down Upper Orwell St and west to Tacket St for the Congregational Church built in 1720 on the site of Christchurch – *not* the mansion of that name. Inside is a headstone to the Rev Will Gordon, minister 1756-64, who became secretary to US President George Washington.

Go west into **Dog's Head St**, named from the *Dog's Head In The Pot* Inn, referring to a hungry dog, not a bizarre menu. The head office of the Ipswich Building Society is on the site, but the nearby *Cock and Pye* pub is still trading where the old cockfighting pit used to be.

St Stephen's St leads to the 15th-cent church of the same name, now in other use. Cross the Old Cattle Market, now the bus station, and Silent St leads to **St Peter's Church**, redundant although the evangelical revival began here in 1801. Ipswich has 12 medieval churches, all built in flint and all but two redundant. St Clement's holds the graves of Thomas Eldred who sailed around the world with Thomas Cavendish of Trimley St Mary, and of Thomas Slade who designed Nelson's flagship *Victory*.

The classic lines of the **Old Customs House**, opened in 1845 in front of the Wet Dock, attract lovers of architecture, and **Isaac Lord's House** in Fore St is a good example of 16th and 17th cent building. From 79 to 83 **Grimwade St** is England's longest bressumer, a horizontal beam supporting masonry over a door or window.

Port and rail. The Ipswich Dock Act of June 1837 established the present dock company and saw the dredging of the Orwell upstream from Pin Mill. The deepwater docks that were built in Ipswich were then the largest in England. But they needed rail links with London – and John Cobbold of the brewing family decided to form the Eastern Union Railway in 1844, linking to Colchester and later to Bury St Edmunds. Stoke Tunnel, leading into the station, was cut in 1846 and is the only one in East Anglia.

The railway and the port brought a great increase in heavy industry, with the gas and coke works, and a coprolite processor, (see Waldringfield) opening in 1849 and a small Fisons fertilizer business moving from Levington in 1850. Rail and river were joint benefactors to the town, but they were such great rivals that in 1871 the Great Eastern Railway agreed to pay a levy on all coal it hauled into town.

Depresson to boom. Depression struck after World War One but the port authority expanded Cliff Quay in 1923-24 regardless. Within three years three oil companies had built bulk storage tanks. Trade increased after World War Two and the growth continues, making Ipswich Britain's number four container port and number six roll-on, roll-off lorry ferry.

Modern industry. Early in the 19th cent Robert Ransome began making a self-sharpening ploughshare. Success led to the creation of Ransomes, Sims & Jefferies, which is now big in the lawn-mower business. Tollemache & Cobbold has been brewing beer for generations, but Ipswich's biggest industry today is insurance. Here is the Guardian Royal Exchange, opposite the **glass offices** of Willis Faber, which has a pool and an acre of lawn on its roof.

Airport. Ipswich Airport, opened in June 1930, was a wartime satellite for RAF Wattisham and RAF Martlesham Heath, operating Blenheim bombers for one and Spitfires for the other. In 1941 it became RAF Ipswich, towing gliders along the coast for target practise for Landguard Fort artillery.

It closed for civilian use in 1946 and, as it never had hard runways, it stayed as a flying club with brief commercial roles as a feeder to Southend Airport, and base in 1986 for Suckling Airways. But the grass gave way in wet weather.

Ipswich Council took it over in 1989 and closed it in 1994..

Ipswich pubs. The borough has more than 100 pubs, but here are a few with unusual names: *Blooming Fuchsia,* Foxhall Rd; *Cock & Pye,* Upper Brook St; *Margaret Catchpole,* Cliffe Lane (named from a smuggler); *Newt & Cucumber,* Falcon St; *Ostrich,* Wherstead Rd; *Toad & Raspberry,* St Peter's St.

Thomas Wolsey's signatures: left, as himself; right as Cardinal, and Archbishop of York.

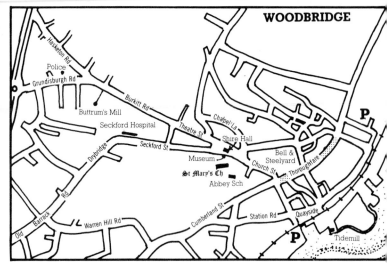

Buttrum's Mill in Woodbridge is the tallest surviving windmill in Suffolk

5: BETWEEN ORWELL and DEBEN

Felixstowe and Woodbridge

RIVERS HAVE BEEN IMPORTANT trade routes and boundaries since the dawn of civilization. The Orwell and the Deben are no exception, but the peninsula between them has no name at all.

In medieval times it was a poor area with small villages on poor soil, which is also true of the land north of the Deben. It was all known as the Sandlings – but Ipswich and Woodbridge, at the head of the estuaries, grew rich on exporting wool, mostly raised on the heavier clays to the west.

To compare the difference in wealth, look at the churches: inland were some of the richest medieval churches in England, but on the coast they were poor. Indeed, the only useful product of the Sandling was fossilized animal dung – **coprolite**.

This peninsula may have remained undeveloped except for the achievements of Admiral Edward Vernon and Colonel George Tomline, but neither made his fortune from the soil.

Admiral Vernon's simple signature.

NACTON

Let us start our discoveries in **St Martin's Church** where an enormous plaque eulogises Sarah Vernon, then adds:

> Sacred to the Memory of EDWARD VERNON, Admiral of the White Squadron of the British Fleet…
>
> …in War with Spain MDCCXXXIX [1739] he took the Fort of Porto Bello with 6 ships…He subdued Chagre & Carthagena… he died as he had lived, the Friend of Man, the Lover of his Country, the Father of the Poor, aged LXXIII.

1739 saw a naval encounter between Spain and England in which Captain Robert Jenkins lost his ear, and so started the War of

Jenkins's Ear. In the war, Admiral Vernon captured Pôrto Belo in Brazil, but couldn't hold it. Later he attacked Sagres (Chagre) in Portugal and Cartagena in Spain, in a conflict which the first Prime Minister, Sir Robert Walpole, did not support. But when Walpole retired in 1742 he was created Earl of Orford.

Grog. Vernon had a habit of wearing a cloak of *gros grain*, corded silk, called 'grogram' in English. It gave him the name Grog Vernon, a word which passed into the language when he watered down the seamen's rum ration to prevent drunkenness. Sadly for some, grog is no longer issued.

Orwell Park. Vernon, Member of Parliament for Ipswich, had Orwell Park mansion built for him in Nacton, and in 1803 the estate hosted England's first steeplechase, from Ipswich barracks to Nacton church.

The original Orwell Park was on a long north-south axis but when George Tomline bought the place in 1857 he realigned it east-west: his initials and the date are on the clock-tower. He bricked up several windows, added a conservatory, orangery, billiard room and ballroom, and the tower where a 10in (25cm) telescope is still in use. And he refaced the building, making it a sumptuous Georgian mansion.

Then he invited the aristocracy to his lavish shooting parties: the Empress of Germany, the Duke of Cambridge, cabinet ministers and industrialists, all came, from 1875 some using Tomline's own railway and his own station at Nacton: the family was so powerful it moved Nacton village away from its mansion.

Tomline's old home at Nacton is now the Orwell Park School

When Tomline died in 1887, Orwell Park and much of the peninsula passed to the Prettyman family of Colchester, soon to be England's richest commoners. And the parties continued. The Prince and Princess of Wales, Winston Churchill... But in 1937 the Prettymans sold out to Aldeburgh School who converted Orwell Park to a public school.

Desert Rats. The 1st Tank Regiment, the `Desert Rats,' were here in 1944 training for the Normandy Landings. In their short stay they smashed the ornate gates and built field kitchens on the cricket pitch – but they helped win the war. Today **Orwell Park School** is a prep school for 200 boys and girls from seven to 13.

Broke Hall. Let's go back·to the church and look at the Broke Chapel. There are plaques to Admiral Sir George Broke-Middleton, high sheriff of Suffolk in 1864; to Lt-Gen Horatio George Broke; to Maj-Gen Sir Charles Broke Vere, wounded in the Peninsular War; and to Rear-Admiral Sir Philip Bowes Vere Broke, who died in 1841. Sir Philip was commander of H.M.S. *Shannon* when he captured the U.S. frigate *Chesapeake* in 1813. But Grog Vernon commanded the British fleet at the Battle of Chesapeake. Sir Philip's victory led to the pub in **Bucklesham** being called the Shannon, while the small cannon in **Levington** supposedly came from the *Chesapeake*. Broke Hall? It's been converted into private flats.

FELIXSTOWE

Whichever way you look at Felixstowe you see a rags-to-riches story, twice over. And it all happened because of an insult.

Col. George Tomline of Orwell Park, wanted to be MP of Harwich, but the townspeople turned him down. Bitterly disappointed, he vowed he would ruin Harwich and Dovercourt, and let the people see it happen.

Bishop Felix. Felixstowe at that time was a tiny neglected village named from Bishop Felix, and Tomline began his campaign by charging the Government for the right to cross his Orwell Park estates to reach **Landguard Fort**, enlarged in 1626.

In 1874 Tomline engaged contractors to begin the Ipswich to Felixstowe railway, although he didn't always have the money to pay wages. Then Charles Parkes, chairman of the Great Eastern Railway, decided to build **Parkeston Quay** outside Harwich: the burghers didn't want his railway in their town. The Harwich Conservancy Board also asked the House of Lords to throw out Tomline's Railway and Pier Bill.

Now twice snubbed by Harwich, Tomline increased his efforts and in 1875 won approval to extend the rail to a pierhead actually in Harwich Harbour.

Felixstowe Dock. Felixstowe Dock, the enclosed basin, was opened in 1887, and in that same year the Great Eastern Railway bought out the new line from Ipswich to Felixstowe, Tomline's masterpiece. But while the commercial side grew, so did the spa. Tomline built the Felixstowe Pier Hotel: it was renamed the Little Ships after World War Two in honour of the motor torpedo boats which berthed in the dock.

Cremation. When Tomline died his dream was well on the way to materialisation. But he hadn't finished with making his name, as his was the first recorded cremation in East Anglia in modern times.

●

SHOTLEY MARINA

Shotley Marina was built in 1987 on the site once occupied by the floating H.M.S. *Ganges*. The marina is unique along the east coast as its 350 berths are accessible at all states of the tide, through a fully-automated lock, 30.3m by 9.09m. Indeed, many skippers visit the marina just to experience the lock.

The marina is ultra-modern with all the facilities that one would expect, such as water and electricity on every berth, diesel sales, 24-hour security, a chandlery and general store, car and cycle hire, and yacht brokerage. The Shipwreck bar and restaurant is fully licensed and able to cater for up to 200 people – and is open to non-sailing non-members. In addition, the marina is home to the renowned Custom Boat Builders and the Ganges Museum.

Shotley Marina hosts the Classic Boat Festival, the largest of its kind in the world, the high spot of which is the Pin Mill Barge Race, starting from Pin Mill and ending in Harwich Harbour, and staged annually around the summer solstice.

Contact: Shotley Marina, Shotley Gate, IPSWICH IP9 1QJ, 01473.788982, fax 788868.

See also page 11.

●

Success. After 1887 the Empress of Germany stayed at Felixstowe with her children, and this regal approval seems to have set the seal on success. In 1902 the promenade was begun, and in 1904 Felixstowe had its pier, a major triumph as neither Harwich nor Dovercourt yet had one. In those days it was fashionable to cruise from London up the Suffolk coast, landing at the piers in Southend, Walton-on-the-Naze and Felixstowe. Eventually Clacton, Southwold and Great Yarmouth would have their piers and join the service.

Also in 1904 Felixstowe Dock had its first big roller mill to take Canadian grain, which marked the beginning of the end for many regional windmills.

Failure. It had been a hectic 30 years. Then the Great War

changed everything. The dock became a base for minesweepers. Edward VIII's yacht was commandeered – but the Harwich Fleet, including 30 battleships and cruisers, used Felixstowe as a coaling station.

After the war, the Great Depression hit Felixstowe more than any other port in England and much of the dock structure fell into ruin. Several 'F' series seaplanes based at Felixstowe had been used for submarine-spotting; now in 1919 an F Fury Trideck with five 375hp engines crashed as it took off on a test flight to India.

●

THE PORT OF FELIXSTOWE.

Quayside cranes (pictured) at the Port of Felixstowe make a spectacular backdrop to the Suffolk coast's southernmost extremity, Landguard Point. Here is one of the most popular visitor attractions in the whole county, with space for 60 cars at a public viewing area between Landguard Fort and Landguard Container Terminal. Whatever the season, hundreds of people enjoy this free viewpoint every day.

Ship spotters among them know that the port works 24 hours a day, seven days a week. It is never closed to the vital task of moving and safeguarding imports and exports.

By far the largest centre of container activity in the British Isles, Felixstowe is linked by 80 shipping lines with 370 ports in 100 countries. It ranks 15th in the world and 4th in Europe.

The port, however, is a much diversified operation. Roll-on roll-off freight ferries sail every few hours to and from the near Continent, and Felixstowe is also a leader in forest products, especially quality paper.

Landguard Terminal pioneered the advent of containerisation in the UK in 1967. Northwards from Tomline's original dock basin, opened in 1886, is the newly-extended Trinity Terminal, with the longest continuous quayline in Britain. Beyond that is the Trimley Nature Reserve, also funded by the port.

See pages 31-44 for the origins of the Port of Felixstowe.

●

It took the Second World War to revive the town. The boom defence depot was here, the RAF had an Air-Sea Rescue base, the Navy's 'little ships' came, and Landguard Fort had two 26ft naval guns. The dock itself became HMS *Beehive*, a base for motor torpedo boats. One of the flotilla commanders was Ian Trelawny who took part in actions in the North Sea and the Channel.

Gordon Parker. Again, it was only a temporary reprieve. By 1951 there was nothing left of the port but a single crumbling wooden jetty, a silting-up dock, and a hinterland of military junk. Into this mess walked Gordon Parker, an East Anglian corn merchant fed up with problems at ports burdened by the National Dock Labour Scheme – but the few facilities were swamped in the 1953 floods. Seeing that as no more than a setback, Parker brought in Trelawny to attract new trade and recruit a workforce willing to learn new ways of cargo handling. Risk-taking management and good labour relations generated substantial private investment for the UK's container revolution to start here at Landguard Terminal, in 1967.The Dock and Railway Company built a 335m (1,100ft) jetty, extended the new container terminal and, by 1973, had a new road access which bypassed the town. Tor Line and Townsend Thoresen began passenger services, and European Ferries took over the Dock and Railway Company.

Statistics tell the next stage: in 1964 Felixstowe handled 376,669 tons of cargo and no containers; in 1990 bulk cargo had reached 16,092,637 tonnes, plus 1,000,929 containers. Then in June 1991 the Hong Kong based Hutchison Whampoa bought 75% of Gordon Parker's child for £100,000,000 and completed the purchase later. The port is the second largest in Britain for roll-on, roll-off traffic, top for imports of quality paper products, a leader for dry and liquid bulk cargos, and a pioneer in the best traditions of free enterprise.

Trimley Marshe Nature Reserve. The reserve, funded by the port and managed by Suffolk Wildlife Trust, attracts ever-increasing numbers of wildfowl, waders and dragonflies. Human visitors are welcome, too.

See page 33 for more on the Port of Felixstowe.

LANDGUARD FORT

The peninsula of Landguard Point has been growing for centuries. It was a small island sandbank when John de Vere, Earl of Oxford, designed a fort for it in 1539 on Henry VIII's orders. Oxford's men came over by boat from Harwich rather than walk down through the marshes of Suffolk, where Felixstowe now stands. Two blockhouses rose in 1543 but were part dismantled in 1552, to be rebuilt in 1588 against the Spanish Armada.

The defences were totally rebuilt between 1625 and '28, and opened fire on a king's ship when its captain refused to dip his flag in salute. The fort was damaged more than the ship.

Dutch landing. Landguard was on trial in the Second Anglo-Dutch War of 1667 when Admiral de Ruyter landed 3,000 men at the foot of Felixstowe cliff and marched 1,000 of them to Landguard. The invasion was brief but it hurt English morale as it was one of the few enemy incursions since 1066. The next year Charles II inspected Landguard, again coming over from Harwich.

By now the sandbank was joined to Suffolk, but it was considered

34

to be part of Essex as it was south of Harwich. Indeed, the fort's postal address was *Landguard, Harwich, Essex,* until the 1950s! Indeed, the peninsula continued to grow with the accumulation of gravel washed down by the sea, and the fort itself was now half a mile from the tip.

Tomline. Landguard Fort was again rebuilt in 1720, with labourers and material coming over from Harwich, but soon a spring was to be found at Walton, near Felixstowe, and its waters taken to the fort by a 5cm (2in) pipe, Landguard's first tangible link with Suffolk. When Tomline was charging the Government for the right to cross his land, he found the pipe, severed it with a spade, and demanded £40,000 for his rights. He was awarded just £2,000, but the Army got a 999-year lease of the pipeline.

The fort was greatly enlarged in 1875 and had 22cm (9in) bore, 12-ton guns added, overlooking the harbour. They were taken out in 1914, the Army relying instead on ordnance mounted outside the fort while 150 men were billeted inside. By now the fort's supplies came from Felixstowe, but the troops were still ferried from Harwich. An unusual touch was that the fort had the rare right to fly the Union flag (the so-called Union Jack) every day, and the Royal Standard on specified days.

Landguard was in control of the boom defence system (an anti-submarine net across Harwich Harbour) and the magnetic mine fields in World War Two. Decommissioned in 1956 it lay derelict until the **Felixstowe History and Museum Society** took it over in 1979.

The twin churches in the twin villages of Trimley

English Heritage owns the building and its 7.5acre (3ha) site, but **Felixstowe Museum** owns the many artefacts on display.

See page 48 for the Felixstowe Museum.

FELIXSTOWE – THE RESORT.

The resort caters for all ages, but has a beach of fine shingle, most of the sand having been carried down to the Thames Estuary. There's a small sandy beach at Felixstowe Ferry, but no more before Lowestoft. The sea front has an amusement park, adventure playgrounds, mini-trains, boating lake, crazy golf, plus an unusual water clock built from scrap metal, alloy from a Concorde wing, and metal from a bomb.

The **Leisure Centre** offers conventional indoor amusements and includes the **Tourist Information Office** at Undercliff Road West, IP11 8AB, 01394.276770. North is the **Spa Pavilion Theatre** which has popular family entertainment in the season.

Shopping. Hamilton Road is the main shopping area, with most national stores represented. **Great Eastern Square** is a shopping precinct using the converted railway station as trains now leave from a platform 100m away.

Ferry to Harwich. For years there was a passenger ferry link to Harwich aboard the *Brightlingsea* ferry. It has closed, leaving no link to Shotley or to Harwich.

FELIXSTOWE FERRY.

This isn't a village, or a hamlet. It's a collection of cafés, of which the **Ferry Café** is open year-round; shops selling fresh or frozen fish; and a public toilet.

Ferry. Mr Weir of Orford runs the ferry to Bawdsey. Nov-Feb, by arrangement; Sep, Oct and Apr, May, weekends and bank hols; Mar, Sundays; June-Aug, daily. In peak season the boat operates on demand 0900-1800 and may carry 450 people in a day. Cycles are also carried. To book the boat call 01394.450637.

Warning. Do not attempt to swim the Deben at Felixstowe Ferry. Except at the turn of the tide, the current is dangerously fast and swimmers would have no chance. It is too fast to row against most of the time.

King's Fleet. In medieval times the Deben emptied into a large basin west of the ferry, where the Ordnance Map shows marshes. The narrow King's Fleet creek is all that remains of this harbour where Edward III gathered his fleet before sailing against Calais in 1346.

NORTH FROM FELIXSTOWE

THE TRIMLEYS. The twin villages of Trimley St Mary and Trimley St Martin offer the rare sight of two churches in the same churchyard. St Martin's has a north chapel built for Roger Cavendish in 1405; he was a forebear of Thomas Cavendish born in 1555 at Grimston Hall, now a farmhouse to the west.

Thomas Cavendish. Thomas squandered most of the family fortune, then joined Sir Richard Grenville's voyage to Virginia in 1585. The next year he used the last of his money to finance his own expedition with the Harwich-built *Desire* of 120 tons, and two other boats. Sailing from Plymouth in 1587, he passed through the Magellan Strait and was soon plundering the Pacific coast. In late 1588 he met the Spanish *Santa Ana* of 700 tons and stole her cargo of silks, wine, and 122,000 gold pesos. He crossed the Pacific and reached England after a voyage of two years, 50 days, making him the second commander to circumnavigate the world.

He sailed again in 1592 but had to turn back at the Magellan Strait, and died before reaching England.

KIRTON

A road in south Kirton usually has a sign warning of the **frog crossing.** Also look for the large sundial on the front of Richmond Cottage in the main street. Ss Mary and Martin's church is rare in having no south door, so you enter through a modern north porch.

FALKENHAM

St Ethelbert's Church lists all the Archbishops of Canterbury from 597 to 1903, but strangely omits Stigand of Hintlesham. Would you like the list to the Norman Conquest?

597 Augustine	731 Tatwin	833 Ceolnoth	990 Siric
604 Laurentius	735 Nothelm	870 Ethelred	995 Elfric
619 Mollitus	741 Cuthbert	890 Plegmund	1005 Elphege
624 Justus	759 Bregwin	914 Athelm	1013 Living
627 Honorius	766 Jaenbert	923 Wulfhelm	1020 Ethelnoth
655 Deusdedit	793 Ethelhard	942 Odo	1038 Eadsige
668 Theodore	805 Wulfred	960 Dunstan	1051 Robert
693 Brihtwald	832 Feologild	988 Ethelgar	

Robert of Jumièges was outlawed in 1052 but kept Papal support, so Stigand's elevation in that year was not recognised in Rome.

Cedar of Lebanon. A large Lebanese cedar stands in the garden next to the church, one of many in the area. Legend claims that Charles I imported a shipload of young plants through Ipswich but lost his head before he could pay for them, so they were sold to the gentry in the neighbourhood.

Falkenham and Kirton creeks had quays for barges during the great days of sail, but nothing now remains.

The elegant Shire Hall on Woodbridge's Market Hill

NEWBOURNE

Can you imagine taking unemployed miners from Durham and Yorkshire and setting them up as smallholders in Suffolk? That's what the Land Settlement Association did in the 1930s, as well as establishing a marketing co-operative. Strangely, the idea worked.

Nowadays most tenants have bought their holdings and, with the demise of the LSA, they have a new co-op: but most of the large glasshouses belong to Notcutts Nurseries of Woodbridge.

Dolls? St Mary's Church looks like an outsize doll's house, with its small south chapel and its tiny flint nave. The soil is good, yet it never produced wealth in the days of the wool trade.

The chancel was re-roofed in 1980, then the hurricane of 1987 demolished the east wall. Look in the north wall near the pulpit for the peculiar go-nowhere staircase. It once led to the rood, the timber separating nave and chancel at roof level, where statues of Christ were mounted until the Reformation had them destroyed.

WALDRINGFIELD

Waldringfield is two villages in one. Life in the main village revolves around All Saints' Church, with its 16th-cent tower, probably paid for by the rector William Coke of the famous Norfolk family.

There were four bells in the tower in 1790 but by 1813 only one remained, the others having been sold for gunmetal in the Napoleonic Wars. The villagers weren't that patriotic – they wanted money to repair the tower, and the war pushed up the value of scrap metal. On the other hand, a legend claims the bells were stolen, and lost in the Deben when the getaway boat capsized.

Coprolite. By 1862 the church was in ruins, like so many others in the Sandlings. Waldringfield's rector, the Rev. T Waller, sold coprolite – fossilized dung – from the glebe lands to pay for the rebuilding. The years 1869-'90 saw the peak of coprolite digging in coastal Suffolk, and there are many worked-out pits in the area. Mr Waller even paid £30 for a barrel organ, which worked out at £1 a tune.

Then there is the other side of Waldringfield, down by the river. When barges were the main means of transport, up to 25 a week would call here, with coprolite their main cargo for loading. Nowadays the pleasure boater has taken over the waterfront, and you might be able to hire a boat for the day.

MARTLESHAM

Martlesham had an experimental air station in 1917 which grew to become RAF Martlesham Heath in World War Two. Its chief claim to fame is that Gp. Capt Douglas Bader, the legless fighter pilot, was based here. In 1973 the Post Office began building a laboratory on the grass runway and now we have the legacy, the **British Telecom Research Station,** a gaunt concrete building with a tower 71.5m (235ft) high. At a cost of £11,000,000 it replaced the old Dollis Hill labs in London, and it was here that Britain's first microchips were made, and optical fibres developed. The place is built to such fine tolerances that one lab is mounted on anti-vibration strips.

Red Lion. On the old A12, the Red Lion pub has a large figurehead, said to have come from a ship wrecked at the Battle of Sole Bay off Southwold.

The BEALINGS

All Saints' Church in **Little Bealings** is one of 22 in Suffolk to have its tower built over the south porch, which means the ringers of the two bells can greet the congregation. The nave is late 11th-cent.

You enter **Great Bealings**'s Church of St Mary through the Tudor north porch, a rarity. The chancel bench-ends have carvings of exotic African wildlife done in 1850, and a plaque remembers Major Edward Charles Moor who was born in 1848 and died in 1934.

Bealings bells. An earlier Major Edward Moor is the link. He served in the East India Company and saw something of Africa, then bought Bealings Hall in 1806. He buried his collection of heathen dolls in a folly in front of the house.

Later he had nine spring-mounted bells installed in the kitchen so he could summon the servants from any room, but on 2 February 1834 the bells began ringing without human intervention and continued intermittently for 54 days, as witnessed by numerous guests. Was there a link between heathen dolls and ringing bells? A descendant who became rector restored the church in the 1840s, and it is his son who is remembered on the plaque.

The church also asks for prayers for Thomas and Margaret Seckford – but see below to know why.

SECKFORD HALL

This Thomas Seckford, who died in 1505, was an ancestor of that other Thomas Seckford, born around 1515 at **Seckford Hall**. Thomas II studied at Cambridge, became a barrister in 1540 and MP for Ipswich in 1550, and again in 1563 and 1572. On Elizabeth's accession in 1558 he was made one of the Masters of the Court of Requests which heard pleas from poor people, and in 1564 the queen gave him the manor of Woodbridge late Priory in return for a donation of £764 8s 4d (42p).

He died in 1587 and, after the last of his line followed in 1672 the hall had mixed fortunes, reaching 1945 in poor condition. Sir Ralph Harwood saved it, converted it into a hotel, and sold it in 1950.

The new owners have continued the conservation, and Seckford Hall is now one of the most delightful Tudor mansions in the country,

The beautifully-restored post mill at Saxted Green

40

retaining its linenfold panelling, beamed ceilings, and façade. One of the four-poster beds was made in 1587, and other furniture has come from Windsor Castle.

WOODBRIDGE

The *Woodbridge Recorder & Wickham Market Gazette* ran banner headlines on 17 August 1939: *The Greatest Discovery Made in England*. It added that *the priceless gold and silver objects from the Sutton Hoo Ship Burial were not treasure trove* – and that meant that Mrs Edith Pretty, JP, was the owner.

Sutton Hoo. Mrs Pretty had bought the Sutton Hoo estate in 1926. In 1938 she decided to investigate the mounds in the grounds, and in two summer digs she had exposed the 24m (80ft) outline of an Anglo-Saxon longship containing the funeral gifts of a king: gold ornaments and coin, silver plate, arms and armour, buckets and dishes of bronze, and the remains of leather cups, drinking horns, and many domestic items, all with a 1939 value of £1,000,000. It was the greatest discovery of its kind in England, but within days Mrs Pretty gave it to the nation, and it's now in the British Museum.

Army damage. On the last day of August Hitler demanded transit rights across Poland to East Prussia, so the Sutton Hoo digs were filled in with bracken. Two days later Germany invaded Poland and on Sunday, 3 September, Britain went to war. The Army took control of the Sandlings, with Sutton Hoo right in the middle of tank manoeuvres. After the ship had lain undisturbed for some 1,325 years, the Army dug a trench through it.

Raedwald. There was no sign of a body in 1939, but recent soil analysis shows an increased level of phosphate in the soil, inferring the bones had decayed. Other researches hint that the ship was the grave of Raedwald, an Anglo-Saxon king who died in 624 or 625.

Open. The Sutton Hoo Society opens the site May-Sep Mon-Fri afternoons, with group bookings or researchers at any time by appointment.

WODENBRIGG?

Despite the grave offerings, Raedwald had accepted Christianity, the first of the Wuffa dynasty to do so. The community of Woodbridge was sacked by the heathen Danes in the 9th cent, and rebuilt, with a charter of 970 being the first recorded mention of the town by name.

And what a name! From Domesday of 1086 to the annals of the Bigod family a century later, the town has been called Udebryge, Wiebryge, Wodebryge and Wudebrige. 'Wooden bridge' is too simple a guess: it was probably Wodenbrigg, the town of the Norse god Woden or Odin.

Medieval Woodbridge. The Bigod family presented the Saxon church, listed in the Domesday survey as *having 19 acres valued at 2s (10p)* to the Priory of the Augustinian canons who lived where the present Abbey School stands beside the church. The priory was here by 1193 and the canons started the market in 1224 despite opposition from Ipswich, but they were so poor they often had to ask the townspeople for help. In 1296 their demand for money to repair the church bells started a riot, and they received just 5s (25p).

St Mary's Church. By the end of the 14th cent the town was thriving from the manufacture of twill and, despite bubonic plague in 1349, was ready to build a larger church. Limestone came by sea and flints overland from Thetford, and by 1450 St Mary's had its 33m (108ft) tower. Did you know that on 15 March 1753 67-year-old Andrew Fosdike went up and down the 133 steps seven times in 27 minutes? Did you know that tar and faggots were kept at the top in Napoleonic times, to give instant warning of a French invasion?

But back to 1537. When the priory was victim to Henry VIII's dissolution of the monasteries, its buildings and land went to Sir Anthony Wingfield. Five years later the original Saxon church was demolished and its site included in the new plot for St Mary's. Then in 1564 Queen Elizabeth granted Thomas Seckford the lands of Woodbridge late Priory, with the name now explained.

Thomas Seckford. Seckford, born at Seckford Hall, was a benefactor to both church and town. He financed the chapel on the north

Snape Maltings, home to the Aldeburgh Festival

aisle, where he was buried in 1588. He rebuilt the Abbey, beginning in 1564 – it is now the Abbey School – and in 1575 gave the town its **Shire Hall**, originally for the petty sessions. The ground floor was bricked up in 1803 but served as a corn exchange until the 1930s.

Seckford had a seamier side, being suspected of fraud, smuggling and piracy, but nothing was proved.

In his last year Seckford founded the almshouses in Seckford St, endowing them with income from his Clerkenwell property in London. The charity's income in 1588 was £112, reaching £3,000 by 1830. Some Clerkenwell property was sold in 1718, and the remainder in 1987 when the Seckford Foundation assets were around £5,000,000, which is being reinvested in the town.

EDWARD FITZGERALD

Woodbridge's other famous character was Edward FitzGerald, 'Old Fitz', born in 1809 at Bredfield Hall two miles north of town. He was an eccentric. Despite the family wealth, which included estates in Ireland as well as Suffolk, Old Fitz often walked through town in summer with his boots around his neck.

In 1860 he married Lucy Barton, but the marriage failed. He took a small flat on Market Hill and went his own way, naming his little boat *Scandal,* 'the staple product of Woodbridge.'

Edward Moor. Edward FitzGerald was a great friend of Major Moor, owner of those haunted Bealings bells. It was this friendship which set Old Fitz on the trail of the mysteries of the Orient, which he never visited. Instead, he found an 11th-cent Persian manuscript and translated it freely into English. He printed 200 copies, but had to sell most at just a penny each (0.41p). Yet it is for this work that FitzGerald is best known today. Its title is *The Rubáiyát of Omar Khayyám,* and this is its best-known verse:

> The Moving Finger writes; and having writ,
> Moves on: nor all thy Piety nor Wit
> Shall lure it back to cancel half a Line,
> Nor all thy Tears wash out a Word of it.

Alfred, Lord Tennyson. Old Fitz was an acquaintance of Lord Tennyson, who was born on the same day. Tennyson, best known for his *Charge of the Light Brigade*, occasionally stayed at The Bull in Woodbridge. The inn has another claim to fame as George Carlow is buried in its stables. Carlow, an ostler (stableman), preferred that to the churchyard.

King's Head. The King's Head is the oldest secular building in town, probably dating from 1490. It began as a meeting-house for the monks of St Mary's Priory, and it still has a few irregular occupants:

43

the ghost of a man in 18th-cent costume usually checks on new licensees, and children's voices have been heard screaming from the top of the stairs.

Bell and Steelyard. Go down New Street for another unusual pub, the Bell and Steelyard. The steelyard is a 17th-cent weighing-machine which projects over the street and was probably used for corn, although Edward III used a similar one in Ipswich for weighing wool. It was last used in 1880 but was tried again in 1959.

Buttrum's Mill. Standing 18m (60ft) to the top of the tower, Buttrum's Mill at 33 Burkitt Rd is the tallest in Suffolk. Its sails turn and the machinery is in place, but it grindeth not. See it Sat and Sun afternoon, or by arrangement with Mr and Mrs Whitworth on 01394.382045.

Probably built in 1836 it last worked in 1928, miller George Buttrum dying in 1937. It stood idle until council restoration in 1950. Milling was done between the four pairs of stones on the third floor and the later roller-mills on the second. The largest moving millstone weighs 750kg (15cwt) and turned at 120rpm clearing the bedstone by the thickness of this page.

The town's other windmill is further down Burkitt Rd, but it is sailless and serves as the office for retirement homes.

Woodbridge Tide Mill. Tide mills are variants of water mills, using water trapped at high tide instead of streams flowing all the time. The first recorded tide mill in Britain was here in Woodbridge, on the site now occupied by the country's last, in working order.

See page 49 for more on the mill.

WOODBRIDGE SNIPPETS

East Anglia was staunchly Parliamentarian during the Civil Wars. One of Cromwell's naval commanders, Peter Pett, married the daughter of the Crown Inn at Woodbridge, and so brought much business to the town. Yet Pett was later one of the men who brought the future Charles II back to England.

The town had a large garrison in 1803 in anticipation of a Napoleonic invasion, with the Duke of Cumberland in command: hence today's Cumberland St. The Prince Regent (the future George IV) and the Duke of Wellington were frequent visitors on their way to **Sudbourne Hall**, as the prince had his eye on Lady Hertford who lived there. In 1817 he dashed from the hall to Woodbridge to see his dying daughter Charlotte, second in succession to the throne. Her death the next day ultimately led to Victoria becoming queen in 1837.

Stage coach. The last stage coach passed through Woodbridge in 1859, replaced by the railway from Ipswich to Lowestoft. The Victorian era initially saw a great increase in wealth for the town so that by 1856, 699 ships called, moving 37,700 tons of cargo, mostly coal in and corn out. But by the century's end the agricultural depression had hit the town badly, its recovery being mainly from modern tourism.

Museum. The small town museum on Market Hill, features Sutton Hoo, Thomas Seckford, the Napoleonic garrison, and other local history. Open Apr-Oct Thur-Sat, 1000-1600; daily in Aug. Fee.

Market day is Thursday.

BEYOND WOODBRIDGE

A tiny village, **Melton,** expanded in Georgian times after the building of the turnpike from Woodbridge, a mile to the south. St Audrey's Hospital was built here in 1765 as a 'house of industry' and later converted to a mental asylum where the concept of therapy was pioneered.

A German flying-bomb destroyed Edward FitzGerald's birthplace in **Bredfield**. There was a castle here once, but no trace of it, or its moat, remains – beyond the name of the local pub, The Castle.

Wuffa, or Uffa, the Anglo-Saxon ancestor of King Raedwald, has left his name in the village of **Ufford.** Oh, yes: there were three fords here until recent times.

The Church of the Assumption was probably the work of Robert de Ufford, 13th-cent lord of the manor under the all-powerful Bigod protection. William Dowsing, who loved smashing churches, came here in 1643 but spared the place. Was he overwhelmed by the large carvings on the roof's hammerbeams, and by the marvellous **font cover**, said to be the most beautiful in the world, and one of the largest? He called it a *Pope's triple crown with a pelican on top* and you can compare notes if you like: the cover is 1.5m (5ft) when collapsed, but expands to 5.4m (18ft), a wonderful achievement for woodcarvers in 1450.

The notice on the door may hold a clue on why Dowsing passed by, for it says *This is a Church where the Catholic Faith is taught...*

Wickham Market. The monks of Ely owned vast tracts of land around Woodbridge, including the estates where Wickham Market now stands, but they gave this property to King Edgar the Peaceful (959-975); two centuries later the Bigods were the owners.

What does the town's name mean? The Romans had a community here, but left nothing with a name. The village is at the head of an estuary, the *vik* of Viking times, but it could also be a Saxon *wic* or settlement. And *ham* is Middle Low German, also meaning a settlement. The *market* is obvious, but it thrived only in the 14th and 15th cents, the name being retained to distinguish this place from the dozen other Wickhams.

All Saints' Church has a strange dormer window midway up its 42m (137ft) steeple. The bell which hangs here may have announced the Sanctus, but it now chimes the hours for the clock, built in 1884.

Akenfield. The village made famous by television, does not exist, but it's based on Charsfield, a few miles west. It's pretty close to Easton Farm Park.

EASTON

It may be only a tiny village, but Easton is remarkable. It has what is claimed to be the world's longest **crinkle-crankle** wall, built by the Earl of Rochford between 1820 and 1830 around Easton Park, the manorial home. This type of wall wriggles in and out like a snake, and is very sturdy, but it's hopeless for marking accurate boundaries.

Rochford. The first Earl of Rochford was Willem Hendrik Nassau, Lord of Zeylesteyn who came to England in 1688 with William of Orange (William III). The manor of Easton, which was the 'eastern' part of Martley in the Domesday survey (and where is Martley today?), owned the entire village from 1066 until the late 19th cent when it was sold off to tenants.

Box pews. All Saints' Church still has two ornate box pews, built by Sir Henry Wingfield, lord of the manor back in 1650. All other pews are box style, but lacking the Wingfield grandeur.

Dowsing. A floor brass to John de Brok is one of three which survived the attentions of William Dowsing, Cromwell's chief church despoiler. Dowsing came here on 27 Feb 1643 and *brake one inscription in brass and 16 superstitious pictures* as well as ordering the parish to *level the steps in 20 days*. Yet the remarkable thing was that Dowsing's family lived in the village and several of them are buried here.

With the Restoration of the Monarchy in 1660 it became compulsory to display the Royal coat of arms in every church: Easton has the Hanoverian arms.

EASTON FARM PARK

The commercial farm extends to some 4,400 acres which, in an average year, can produce some 2,500,000 pints of milk, 7,000 tonnes of cereal, 5,000 of potatoes, 1,300 of beet sugar, and 500 tonnes of peas and beans for freezing. But around 150 acres (60ha) are devoted to the tourist attraction of **Easton Farm Park – see page 56 for full details.**

6: BETWEEN DEBEN and ALDE

Medieval castles and radar

WIDFORD BRIDGE, crossing the Deben, takes its name from the wildfowling formerly done here. And the gentle hill behind the next roundabout is called **Gallows Hill** for obvious reasons. The golf club on the site has Gallows Hole as one of its 18, and skulls have been found in the sand of the old club house car park.

The Woodbridge garrison preparing for Napoleon had troops stationed here, with one of their commanders being Sir John Moore who won the Battle of Corunna but is slightly better remembered for a poem about his death there:

> Not a drum was heard, not a funeral note,
> As his corpse to the rampart we hurried;
> Not a soldier discharged his farewell shot
> O'er the grave where our hero we buried.

Head south on B1083, passing the entry to the **Sutton Hoo** site and venturing deep into the Sandlings, an area suitable only for sheep grazing, and not much good at that.

Sutton. Sutton is a sprawling parish that includes some of the base of RAF Woodbridge, a victim of the end of the Cold War. It's blissfully peaceful now the aircraft have gone – but so have the jobs. The church tower collapsed in 1642 and was never repaired.

SHOTTISHAM

Some people think that Edmund, King of East Anglia and the first patron saint of England, was slain here in 870. Others place the event at Hoxne, pronounced *Hocksun*. Take your pick.

Wood Hall. Wood Hall is a Tudor manor house built in 1566 and now standing in 10 acres (4ha) with a walled garden and a lake. The Domesday survey lists the manor as the property of Gilbert, Bishop of Evreux, and valued at £12. Later records show the hall was rebuilt in 1675 for £4,000, and that more recently it was owned by **Sir**

Thomas Cuthbert Quilter. 1st Baronet Bawdsey. The Dowager Lady Quilter refurbished the manor in 1906, but it is now the **Wood Hall Hotel** and country club.

A girl, staying in room 17 around 1910, fell into the lake and was never seen again, but her ghost has been back, seen and heard in the upper corridor looking for her parents and bouncing a ball. Previous owners often saw their spinning wheel turning without visible power, but the most unusual ghost is that of a stallion which strangled itself on a hitching post, and has reappeared in the grounds. Is there any connection with the thatched pub, the Sorrel Horse?

●

FELIXSTOWE MUSEUM

Situated in Landguard Fort, the Felixstowe Museum has 10 display rooms offering a vast range of artefacts from Roman times to the present, including an 18th-cent whipping post. Housed in a fort built mainly in 1878 by the Royal Engineers, the museum features the history of the town as well as the fort itself, with emphasis on Landguard Point and its outbuildings in World War Two, under Army, Naval and Royal Air Force occupation.

Opening times are 2pm to 5pm, Sun and Wed, late May to late Sep. Thurs, during summer school holidays. No unaccompanied children. Guided tours of the fort exterior. Light refreshments available; nearest toilets on Manor Terrace car park.

See page 34 for Landguard Fort.

●

ALDERTON

Alderton's church tower collapsed in the 18th cent, demolishing much of the nave. The nave was re-roofed in 1864-65 but the tower was never rebuilt, another proof of the relative poverty of the area. An earlier rector sent his gardener with a bowl of soup every Saturday morning to the poor of the parish – but only if they were in church the previous Sunday. And in slightly later times the manors of Alderton, Bovils, Peckys and Earl Alderton appointed the rector in turn, presumably because no single manor could undertake the burden permanently.

RAMSHOLT. The village of Ramsholt is remote and tiny, nestling on the Deben foreshore, but its pub, the Ramsholt Arms, was a ferry house and is still a good excuse for mooring your boat at the quay until the tide turns. Barge traffic, sadly, has given way to pleasure craft.

The windmill at Thorpeness (above) used to pump water to the House In The Clouds. Below, militaria in the Felixstowe Museum

WOODBRIDGE TIDE MILL

One of Suffolk's best known landmarks, the tide mill stands in a prominent position on the busy Woodbridge quayside and is much photographed by visitors who pass through its doors during bank holidays and the summer months.

There has been a tide mill in Woodbridge for more than 800 years, but the present building dates from 1793. In 1564 Queen Elizabeth I presented the earlier mill to Thomas Seckford, the town's greatest benefactor.

The tide mill finished its working life in 1957 and shortly after, the 7.5acre tidal pond was sold to a local boatyard to be used as a marina. This sale was unquestionably the most significant factor in ensuring the mill would never work commercially again.

Indeed, by 1967 it was in such a sorry state that it seemed destined to follow the fate of other tide mills. However, its fortunes changed when Mrs Jean Gardner of Wickhambrook created a trust for its restoration, and eventually presented it to Woodbridge Town Council. The mill continues to be administered by a trust to this day. Due to trust members' efforts and those of the Friends of the Tide Mill, it was completely restored in the mid 1970s and has opened to the public on a regular basis ever since.

See page 44 in the main text.

●

BAWDSEY

Sir William Cuthbert Quilter was born in London in 1841. He became a stockbroker at 22 which set him on course to make a fortune. At 26 he married a Suffolk woman and turned his interest to the Woodbridge area, renting Hintlesham Hall, buying Wood Hall, and other lands until he had 8,000 acres; his descendants still own much of it. Land was cheap because of the agricultural depression, and the Sandlings were sheapest of all.

He also bought the manorial lordship of Bawdsey, where the church tower had collapsed and the nave was derelict. Little remained of the village, the former Saxon community called *Baldhere's Island*.

Bawdsey Manor. Quilter bought his first yacht in 1871, from Edward FitzGerald, and in 1875 he became vice-commodore of the Royal Harwich Yacht Club. He started building Bawdsey Manor in 1886, financing it from Quilter, Barlfour & Co, stockbrokers, and finishing it in 1904. A story claims that he added a tower for every £1,000,000 he made. There are nine towers, and he left £1,200,000 in cash in 1911.

Great Eastern Square in Felixstowe is a colourful shopping precinct

The interior was lavish, with panelling from an ocean liner, and an organ which is now in Ramsholt Church. The vegetable garden was tended by Percy Thrower's father.

But life at the manor was not easy. Quilter, MP for Sudbury 1885-1906, ruled with Victorian rigidity; children may speak only when spoken to, and any employee found malingering would be sacked. Yet Quilter created jobs where there were none, and provided the first steam-powered ferry across the Deben's mouth.

R.A.F Bawdsey. Meanwhile, **Sir Robert Alexander Watson-Watt** had been working on the idea of radio detection and ranging – radar – at Orford Ness since May 1935 but, as the site was becoming unsuitable, the Government bought Bawdsey Manor from the second Baronet Quilter in 1936 for £24,000, and the radar team moved here in total secrecy in February 1936. Radar development was so secret that Arthur Ransome referred to 'tall wireless masts' in *We Didn't Mean To Go To Sea* published in 1937.

The R.A.F. and Sir Robert worked hard on radar, and by the outbreak of war in 1939 Britain had 19 radar stations on the east coast and six on the south, and on the first night of war, 3-4 September, a Blenheim bomber was flying over London with a miniature radar aboard. Hours after the plane landed, radar research moved to Dundee, but the work at Bawdsey helped win the war and radar stayed secret until 16 August 1945.

Bawdsey remained a radar station until 1974, then from 1979 until its closure in 1991 it was a Bloodhound missile base, although 99m (325ft) of one mast remains for the BBC's ship to shore service. The manor was sold in 1994 for conversion to the Alexanders International School, teaching English to foreigners, with a radar museum planned.

Goseford. Bawdsey, an island in Saxon times, had a sandbank link to the mainland by the Middle Ages, with a large harbour at the mouth of the Deben, opposite King's Fleet and known as Goseford. It was a major port for the wool trade and a second haven for the king's fleet. Bawdsey's church tower, of unknown height before losing its top, was a major landmark. The Augustinian friars of Butley Priory appointed Bawdsey's priests until the Dissolution.

Hollesley. Pronounced *hoal-zee*,the tiny village is best known for its penal colony, built to hold 384 young inmates. It stands in 1,700 acres which include a dairy farm.

SHINGLE STREET. Shingle Street is one of the most isolated communities in Suffolk, and popular because of it. It was a sea-bathing and shipping hamlet in the early 19th cent, although I cannot imagine how anybody could swim off the steep shingle beach, with a rip tide surging up or down the Ore; it's 16.8km (10.5miles) by river to Slaughden, and much of this water is emptied at every tide. A mile of the southern tip of Orford Ness was destroyed in 1898 and the peninsula changes continually.

War. During the war, troops practised landing on a hostile beach, but Shingle Street proved far too hostile and hundreds of men were burned to death. The story was supressed until recently, and even then was officially denied.

Boyton. You might call in at the church to see the book of rules, with suggested forfeits for those who break them.

BUTLEY

Butley is a tiny village near the head of the Butley River, where oyster farming was recently reintroduced. Only the gateway survives of Butley Priory, founded in 1171 for the Augustinians. In the mid-19th-cent Thomas Crisp of Abbey Farm sent cattle abroad by the train-load, and a later resident exported lupin seeds to Belgium, where they were used to make dye.

Call in at **Butley Pottery** in Mill Lane, established by Honor Hussey in 1980 who produces hand-thrown bowls, pots and urns, on sale here and in other outlets. Operating from a barn built in 1795 and now restored, the Husseys also run the Barn Gallery and the Tea Barn, for snacks or five-course banquets. Open daily Apr-Sep, Wed-Sun Oct-Mar. Bed and breakfast is a possibility.

The Ore at Orford: beware the current at mid-tide

The FORESTS

By now we have almost circled **Rendlesham Forest** which, with **Tunstall Forest** to the north-east, and **Dunwich Forest** north of Leiston, was very severely damaged by the hurricane of 17 October 1987. The three plantations are collectively known as Aldewood Forest and before the storm Rendlesham covered 3,958 acres (1,602ha), Tunstall 3,064ac (1,240ha), and Dunwich 1,650ac (666ha). Collectively it is a long way short of England's largest forest at Thetford, which has 51,500ac (80sq miles, 208sq km).

Aldewood was nothing more than poor grazing land until afforestation began in 1920. The plantations specialise in Scots pine, with lesser Corsican pine and Douglas fir; oak and poplar never thrived in the poor sand. By 1972 17,000 cu m – 17,000 tonnes – of wood were being harvested each year for woodwool or pulp. Then came the hurricane, which flattened vast areas within an hour, closing roads for days.

EYKE

In Saxon times an oak forest grew above the Deben valley, the name of the tree living on in the name of the village, Eyke. Legend claims that Staverton Park, towards Butley, has oaks 1,000 years old.

Eyke was not mentioned in Domesday but we know that in that year, 1086, Hubert de Monte Caniso (not 'Casino'), better known as the Munchensi, held the manor of **Staverton.** Late in the 12th cent Ralph de Munchensi gave Hugh Bigod, the future Earl of Norfolk, the

Staverton manor. The Bigods passed it to the Stavertons, earls of Suffolk, and it was John de Staverton who, in 1381, saw an offshoot of the Peasants' Revolt break into his manor and steal the documents which proved serfdom.

Staverton was appointed Baron of the Exchequer in 1399, and after his death the estate passed to the Alraids. Thomas Alraid was one of Cromwell's many servants, but the family let the hall fall into decay and today nothing survives.

Seckford. The villagers of Eyke revolted against **Thomas Seckford** in 1587 because he threatened to fine them if they wore German style felt hats in church. The villagers wore the hats, and were fined.

Another revolt was in 1644 against the rector, Nicholas Stoneham who, the villagers claimed, was *a common alehouse and tavern haunter* who *hath been present camping on the Lord's Day*. Camping was a game like rugby but without the ball. Mr Stoneham? He was sacked.

Unusual church. Eyke's towerless and spireless church is unique in eastern England. The choir is in the west; the font, organ and pews in the east, and the pulpit in the centre. The first recorded **pub** was there in 1518, and was later owned by John Cobbold, a family name big in modern brewing. By 1639 it was the Crown Inn, but John Fuller converted a private house in 1707 and moved the pub to there, calling it the Elephant and Castle – owned today by Tolley Cobbold.

Rendlesham. Little survives of Rendlesham village, and not a trace has been found of the Uffa or Wuffa royal hall, believed to have been here. Its owner was Raedwald, believed buried at Sutton Hoo.

TUNSTALL. St Michael's spacious church in Tunstall still has its box pews, looking like third-class open-topped railway carriages from George Stevenson's time, but now historically important. A single brass remains, dated 1618, probably spared Dowsing's wrath because it bears no human image. The Great War memorial tells of 625 villagers of whom 131 went to war, and 18 never came home.

The Growing Stone. There's a lovely story about the large boulder in the front yard of Stone Farm, **Blaxhall**. Legend says it was the size of a football a century ago, but it keeps growing. The farmer, who's proud of what is really a stone brought down in the Ice Ages, believes it to be the largest boulder in Suffolk.

Campsea Ashe. The village of Campsea Ashe lies in the parish of Campsey Ash – note the spelling – where the 14th-cent Church of St Andrew has a tower 23m (76ft) tall. The little spire on top was damaged in the 1987 hurricane and 1989 gales, and was repaired in 1991. Inside, a brass showing the first rector, Alexandre Inghllysh (English), may be the only record we have of a priest's vestments in 1312.

IKEN

Iken has no shop, no pub, no school, no bus service, no phone box, and less than half a dozen houses. But it has a church, which is on one of the oldest sites in England.

Butwulf. Butwulf was a wandering preacher looking for a home. In 647 he found wild woods overlooking a reedy marsh, and got royal permssion to build a monastery there. He became the first abbot, and the first person in Britain to follow the code of St Benedict. The Saxon Chronicle said in 654 that *...in the year King Anna was slain...Botulf began to timber that minster at Ycean-ho.* The evil spirits who inhabited the place – probably will-o'-the-wisp on the marshes – gave terrifying groans and caused a noxious vapor to be emitted from the ground. They had dwelt there for ages, and had nowere else to go, they told Butwulf. Botolph (modern spelling) gave the sign of the cross and set them to flight.

Botolph's church was dedicated to St Martin – not St Benedict – and changed to Botolph himself ages later. The church at Iken is known to be one of the first in eastern England, although the original fell victim to Danish raiders.

The world was singing Botolph's praises: certainly his name was known from Scotland to Pembroke and ultimately to Schleswig where the Slesvig Breviary has a prayer for St Botolph's Day, 17 June.

The holy man died in 680 and was buried at Iken – the name probably comes from the Iceni tribe – his bones being removed between

Iken's original church was one of England's oldest

963 and 975 to Grundisburgh and then, with the remains of St Jurmin (German) to Bury St Edmunds between 1044 and 1065.

Second church. The second church at Iken was built of stone, probably in the 10th cent, yet there is no mention of Iken in the Domesday survey. It next appears in history when Sir William de Esturmy seized it from the Earl of Lancaster in 1297, and built the third church. This was severely damaged by fire in July 1968, but 12 devoted parishioners raised £23,000 to restore the fabric.

CHILLESFORD. People digging for brick-clay at Chillesford found the skeleton of an 18m (60ft) whale, which shows the area was once under water. Some of the bricks in St Peter's Church are believed to be Roman, and a coin of Constantine the Great has been found in the parish.

The Caravan Club runs a camping site beside the church, with no intervening fence. But for a touch of real Suffolk idiosyncracy, look at the local pub, the *Froize Inn.* Froize is an old word for 'pancake.'

SUDBOURNE. All Saints' Church stands remote from the village, which moved for reasons long forgotten. The 19th-cent restoration put a heavy Victorian stamp on the church, but also revealed a hoard of silver coins under the floor, minted in the time of Henry I, Henry II and John.

Saxon pilgrims used an earlier church on this site as a dormitory on their way to visit a local hermit.

ORFORD

Orford Castle. The village of Orford has the impressive remains of one of the most important castles of medieval England, and the oldest for which full accounts have been preserved. Between 1165 and 1173 the cost was £1,413 9s 2d (46p) at a time when a working man earned a penny (0.4p) a day and the Royal exchequer may have been £10,000 a year. More than £663 of that was spent in the first year.

Royal blunder. Henry I had given the manor of Framlingham to Roger Bigod in 1101, and Stephen (1135-54) had given Bigod's son Hugh the earldom of Norfolk, which was putting too much power in the hands of one baron, as the Bigods already held the castles at Thetford and Walton (near Felixstowe, but long eroded), and Bigod began building Bungay Castle in 1164.

Henry, who had only Eye, Colchester and Norwich – and Bigod claimed the latter – began building Orford in 1165. He appointed as viewers – foremen – Robert de Valoines and Bartholomew de Glanville; both were related to Ranulf de Glanville, founder of **Leiston Abbey** and **Butley Priory.** Henry was also improving Orford harbour and the church. Work finished just in time, for in 1173 the barons, including Bigod, revolted. Henry managed to put down the uprising with Church help, and Bigod paid a ransom to keep his castle at Bungay.

In 1216 Henry III became king at the age of 10, though Prince Louis of France had many supporters. Louis attacked eastern England, briefly capturing the castles at Orford, Hedingham and Colchester; it was the only time Orford played any role in English history, for Edward III gave it to the Earl of Suffolk in 1337 and it remained in private hands until 1930 when it was given to the Orford Town Trust.

See page 57 for Orford Castle today.

See page 57 for Orford Castle today.

●

EASTON FARM PARK

Set in the picturesque Deben valley, with Victorian model farm buildings put up by the Duchess of Hamilton around 1870, Easton Farm Park is home to many breeds of farm animals, including Red Poll cattle, Suffolk Punch horses, and Suffolk sheep – the 'Suffolk trinity.'

The park is part of a larger working farm, and the purpose-built dairy centre enables visitors to watch the cows being milked during the afternoon.

The collection of early farm machinery gives a glimpse of life as it used to be. Among the displays of country bygones is a Ransomes Simms and Jefferies threshing machine, and portable steam engine 'Little Ben,' built in 1886.

There's an octagonal Victorian Dairy, still with the original patterned tiles and marble shelves. A Food and Farming exhibition explains food production from the farm to the table over the past 150 years. Children enjoy meeting and greeting the smaller animals in the Pets Paddock. The Green Trail takes visitors along the banks of the Deben and beside the paddocks where sheep and cattle can be seen grazing.

The Tearoom serves a selection of snacks, lunches and teas, and there are selections to be made in the Gift Shop. Special events are held throughout the season, from mid March to late September, 1030 to 1800. Free parking. Contact 01728.746574 for more details and admission rates.

Picture shows part of a Suffolk Horse Spectacular.

See also page 46 of the main text.

See also page 46 of the main text.

●

St Bartholomew's Church. Orford church, rebuilt in the 14th cent beside the ruins of Henry II's original, has an impressively large nave and aisles that flow into one enormous hall, more than adequate

Orford Castle is the oldest fortification in England to have its building costs recorded in detail for posterity. Framlingham Castle *(below) is certainly old; Mary was proclaimed Queen here in 1553.*

ORFORD CASTLE

Orford Castle has an almost perfect keep, while the bailey (the outer walls) collapsed one night in 1841, leaving the large and impressive ditches.

The keep, standing 30m (100ft) high, has 18 facets to its sides, topped by square turrets, and it houses a labyrinth of passages and rooms. At basement level there is the 10m (32ft) deep well; the airy lower hall has the kitchen and lavatory leading off, with all waste going through holes in the masonry to accumulate outside. Slightly higher, the chapel is hidden in a corner buttress. The upper hall had another kitchen and lavatory, with a rainwater cistern above.

Access to the castle keep is up 20 outside steps, with another 91 to the top. At roof level, the rooms in the three turrets are not open, but one holds a bakery with what may be England's oldest glazed floor tiles.

There is a splendid display showing Orford Castle in relation to the town, and the southward growth of the Orford Beach shingle spit which gradually cut off the town from useful access to the sea.

The Ministry of Works took over the castle in 1962 and now, as English Heritage, opens it to the public 1 April-Sep 1000-1800 daily, 1000-1600 at other times.

See page 55 for the history of Orford Castle.

●

FRAMLINGHAM CASTLE

Framlingham Castle is the opposite of Orford: it has one of the best baileys (curtain walls) in England, but it does not appear to have had a keep (the main defense). One of the main attractions of Framlingham is that visitors can walk around the entire curtain wall at battlement level, passing through or around the 13 towers, and look either outward at the countryside, or inward at the walls themselves and the flint-and-brick building in the courtyard.

This was erected in 1729 as a poorhouse, using child labourers in part, who received two hours of schooling a day. The building stayed in use until the Wickham Market workhouse opened in 1839, after which it saw service as a courtroom and fire station until Pembroke College, the owner, gave the castle to the State in 1913.

The original buildings inside the bailey were destroyed in the 17th cent to provide building material for a college and almshouses in the town. The will, which gave the castle to Pembroke College, Cambridge and decreed this act of destruction, was contested for 30 years. One of the results was the delay in putting up Pembroke's Chapel, designed by Wren.

Both Framlingham and Orford castles have small gift shops, and the same opening times, 1 April-September 1000-1800, 1000-1600 at other times.

Picture shows the castle walls and the mere.

See pages 61-63 for the history of Framlingham Castle.

●

to hold the entire population of 1,000 in 1327 as well as today's inhabitants, yet this was long considered the lady chapel for the smaller church at Sudbourne. Several of Benjamin Britten's works had their first public performance here, and it frequently features in the Aldeburgh Festival schedule.

Past glories. In Tudor times the gravel spit was much shorter and ships could moor near the church. So there were 16 warehouses, including the present Crown and Castle Hotel and the Jolly Sailor and King's Head pubs. The Crown and Castle is now the only hotel for miles.

Elizabeth I granted the town its charter in 1579, and it had a mayor until 1886, and *two* MPs until 1852. Now, even the market has gone (it's a car park), the church lost the top of its tower (it's been rebuilt), and the Augustinian Friary and both medieval hospitals have gone.

The Orford Merman. Around 1151 some fishermen caught a man in their nets. Naked and hairy, he was taken to the castle (which was begun in 1165, you remember) where he ate only fish (another version says he ate anything) but would not speak even when hung by his heels. The locals took him back to sea, surrounded by a net, but he dived under and escaped.

Then there was Richard Grey who, in 1793, decided to tell East Anglia that witchcraft was a myth. Few people believed him and in Orford they reacted so violently that they tied him to a stake and piled brushwood around it. Grey escaped and vowed never to return to this horrible town. He settled in Aldeburgh and drowned there in 1861, aged 80.

Havergate Island. Downstream from town is Havergate Island, a nature reserve 3km (2 miles) long and managed by the RSPB, to whose warden you must apply for access: 30 Mundy's Lane, Orford. The launch *October Storm* takes guided tours from Orford on selected days Apr-Aug. The island is where the avocet returned to breed in Britain in 1947.

Cruises. The *Lady Florence,* a 35-ton cruiser plies the river from Orford to Aldeburgh or to Shingle Street, depending on the tide. Call 01394.450897 or mobile 0831.698298 for the master, John Haresnape. *Britannia II* and *Regardless* run cruises around Havergate Island; the former was a jolly-boat on the royal yacht.

ORFORD NESS

The 'island,' as Orford people call the ness, is the loneliest place in East Anglia. Until 1993 it was out of bounds, but the secret establishments have closed, the National Trust has taken over, and people are welcome again – but no more than 96 a day and then only on set days.

The Foreign and Commonwealth Office still holds the northern bulge of the ness and the Nature Conservancy the southern spur, with the National Trust holding the middle.

Airstrip. The story begins in 1915 when an airstrip was built on the ness's marshy land by Stony Creek. As military aircraft outgrew this strip they moved to Martlesham Heath. Later the Ministry of Supply and the Royal Aeronautical Establishment took over, allowing Sir Robert Watson-Watt to begin his radar experiments here in 1935; he moved on to Bawdsey, but the crew of the Italian bomber which attacked the ness in 1941 had no idea of its importance. The plane was shot down on the gravel spit.

Atomic bomb. The Atomic Weapons Research Establishment at Aldermaston took over from the RAE in 1959 to begin testing the trigger mechanism of nuclear bombs, and pulled out in 1971.

Overlapping with the AWRE was an Anglo-American experiment to develop an early warning system under the code name of Cobra Mist. It was planned to supercede Fylingdales in Yorkshire and even the Distant Early Warning Line in Canada. But it didn't work, so Cobra Mist ended in 1973.

BBC. The BBC was the latest arrival, settling in the northern bulge and creating a maze of antennae looking on the map like part of a pie chart. It is the **World Service** transmitter for Eastern Europe.

Lighthouse. Through all the coming and going, Orford Ness had kept its lighthouse. The first one was built of wood in 1603, and burned coal for a beacon. Not surprisingly, it burned down. Two lights replaced it but after the present tower was built in 1792 the lower light was scrapped. The lighthouse is not open to the public.

See page 72.

THE A12 AND WEST

Glemham Hall. Since the death of Lady Blanche Cobbold in 1987, Glemham Hall has not been open to the public. The Georgian mansion was built by the Glemham family who first appear in records in the reign of Henry III.

WIND and WATER MILLS

Few wind or water mills survived the 20th cent; fewer still are working. One of the best-restored water mills is between Easton and Letheringham. **Letheringham Mill**, built around 1740, was almost derelict when Rod and Hilary Allen bought it. The undershot wheel and the interior are new, in the original masonry. The wheel turns at a variety of speeds but lacks the stones that grind the wheat, but come and enjoy the picture gallery, the tea-room, and see the peacocks in the five-acre (2ha) gardens.

Open most Sundays Apr-Sep (not June), 1400-1800. Donation for hospice. 01728.746349.

Saxtead Green Mill. The windmill at Saxtead Green is a splendid post mill, in which the entire structure turns on a central post. A mill was standing here in 1287, one of the earliest in the country as the idea of windpower was brought back by returning Crusaders. This particular mill was here in 1796 and it ground its last corn – for animal feed – in 1947. The Ministry of Works took it over in 1951, restored it between 1957 and '61, and since 1984 English Heritage has been the owner.

It's 14m (46ft) tall, with sails 16.7m (54ft 9in) in diameter. The mill is in working order but the upper stone has been removed for demonstration purposes. Open Easter-Sep, Mon-Sat, 1000-1800; fee. Park in layby 100m west.

FRAMLINGHAM

Framlingham today is a large village, but in earlier times it was a major power in the royal fortunes. You'll probably begin your tour on Market Hill (market on Sat) as the town was an important agricultural market even before the Norman Conquest. Framlingham merchants built the first mill at Saxtead Green.

FRAMLINGHAM CHURCH

The Church of St Michael, rebuilt in the 15th and 16th cents and including part of the 12th cent chancel, is large enough to be the cathedral of a medium-sized city. Go straight to the east end chancel and see what is claimed to be **the most heavily gilded tomb in Europe.** It is for Henry Howard, the poet Earl of Surrey, and of Frances, his countess, although it was probably built in the reign of James I (1603-'25), for the earl was beheaded.

He had been talking too freely about his cousin, Catherine Howard, whom Henry VIII had executed in 1542 after 18 months of marriage. In December 1546 Surrey and his father, Thomas, third Duke of Norfolk, were imprisoned in the Tower of London. Henry redrafted his will, then had Surrey beheaded on 19 January 1547 with his father to follow on the 28th. But in the early hours of that day Henry died, aged 55, and so Norfolk's life was spared.

Other tombs. Nearby is a small tomb for Elizabeth, Surrey's granddaughter, fathered by the fourth Duke of Norfolk: he was executed in 1572.

The Moot Hall at Aldeburgh was built in the town centre but is now on the beach.

Two large plain tombs are for Henry FitzRoy, bastard son of Henry VIII (*fils du roi*, 'son of the king', was reserved for bastards); and his wife Mary, sister of the executed Surrey.

Two wives. The next holds two of the wives of the 4th Duke of Norfolk, beheaded in 1572. The first wife was Lady Mary FitzAlan, daughter of the Earl of Arundel, and it was through this union that the dukes of Norfolk eventually moved to Arundel Castle. The second wife was daughter of Thomas, Lord Audley, Lord Chancellor of England. Her son was Lord Thomas Howard who commanded the fleet when Sir Richard Grenville attacked the Spanish in 1591. The third wife was to have been Mary Queen of Scots, who was to marry him after he deposed Elizabeth and put her on the throne of England. The plan misfired, which is why the duke lost his head.

The last major tomb is for the third Duke of Norfolk, left in the Tower after Henry VIII died. Queen Mary released him in 1553 and he died of natural causes the next year.

A wall plaque commemorates Sir Robert Hitcham, born in Levington, owner of Framlingham Castle in 1635-'36, and attorney to Queen Anne. He *dyed the 15th day of Avgvst Anno 1636.*

FRAMLINGHAM CASTLE

Henry 1 gave Roger Bigod the manor of Framlingham in 1101, and Stephen created his son Hugh Bigod the first Earl of Norfolk in 1140. Hugh began converting a fortified manor house into a castle to join those he had at Thetford, Bungay and Walton.

Henry II managed to deprive Hugh of some of the castles in 1154, including Framlingham, but had to hand them back in 1164. Bigod was one of the leaders of the Barons' Uprising, protesting about Henry's inability to understand his family, of all reasons. Prince Henry (later Henry III) had fled to his French father-in-law, later joined by his brother Richard, Duke of Aquitaine (soon to be Richard I).

Bigod had to surrender Framlingham and Bungay, and the royal engineer demolished Framlingham Castle, which at that time was probably just the fortified manor house.

Hugh's son Roger regained the castle site in the 1180s and gradually rebuilt it during the reign of Richard I. He did not support Richard's successor John, although the duke entertained his monarch at Framlingham in 1213. By now the bailey and 13 towers were complete, much as you see them today, and Framlingham probably never had a keep. John's fortunes went from bad to worse – he lost territories in France, was excommunicated, and forced to sign Magna Carta – so Bigod and his allies offered the crown to Prince Louis of France. While Louis attacked Orford, King John attacked Framlingham. The castle was poorly defended and surrendered after two days, but John died of dysentery the next year, and the regent to the new monarch, 10-year-old Henry III, returned Framlingham to the Bigods.

Edward I ordered Roger Bigod to fight in Gascony while he himself went to Flanders, but Bigod refused. "By God, sir Earl, you will go or hang," Edward thundered. "By God, O King, I will neither go nor hang," replied Bigod. He stayed. But when he died, Edward seized his title and estates.

Duke of Norfolk. Richard II created the Norfolk dukedom in 1397, making Thomas Mowbray the first title holder and giving him Framlingham. The second duke died from the common complaint of the aristocracy, beheading, and further down the line Ann Mowbray was betrothed to Richard, one of the two Princes in the Tower in 1483. Anne later married into the Howard family while the last male Mowbray lost his head to an axe.

Howard. With the Norfolk title and the Framlingham estates in Howard hands, John Howard set about repairing the castle, but was killed at the Battle of Bosworth in August 1485. His son rebuilt Framlingham Church around 1540: and that's where we came in, for this was the man whose execution was cancelled when Henry VIII died.

Queen Mary. Edward VI inherited Framlingham Castle, which he gave to his sister Mary shortly before he died, aged 15. Mary moved in, expecting to hear herself proclaimed queen in accordance with Henry VIII's will – but Edward had annulled the document, leaving Lady Jane Grey, daughter of the Duke of Suffolk, to be proclaimed on 6 July 1553. Thousands of Mary's supporters were camped around

Framlingham and their demands led to Mary being proclaimed on 19 July.

As bees and wasps know, there cannot be two queens, and in 1554 poor Lady Jane, the 13-day monarch, lost her head. Mary let the dust settle before releasing Norfolk from the Tower, and Framlingham faded from the political scene.

Prison. In Elizabeth's time (1558-1603) the castle served as a prison for priests who refused to accept the Church of England's doctrine. James gave the place back to the Howards in 1613 but they never used it, and sold it in 1635.

Robert Hitcham. Sir Robert Hitcham, MP, whose plaque is in the church, bought it, leaving it almost at once to Pembroke College, one of the smallest in Cambridge. And Pembroke gave it to the State in 1913

See page 57 for Framlingham Castle today.

THE TOWN

On Market Hill, **The Crown Hotel** is a good example of Tudor architecture, and served as a post house in the 18th cent. Hitcham's college and almshouses survive nearby.

Railway. 1 June 1859 was a great day. The East Suffolk Railway's branch lines to Snape, Aldeburgh and Framlingham opened. The Framlingham spur, 9km (5.6 miles) long, had five trains a day in each direction in 1883, and six at its peak in 1938, but speed limits laid it wide open to competition from road transport. The last passengers were carried on 3 November 1952 and the freight stopped on 19 April 1965.

'Jane the Quine' wrote Lady Jane Grey, England's shortest-reigning monarch.

'Marye the quene' wrote Jane's successor. Where did they learn to spell?

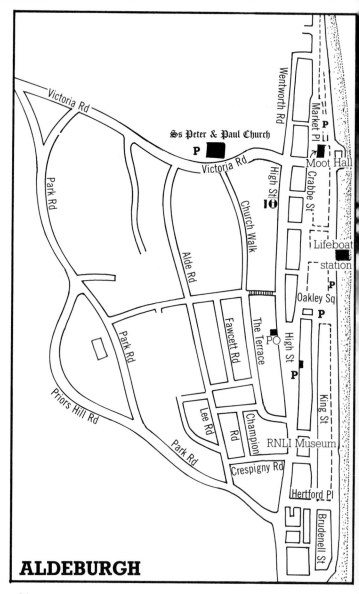

ALDEBURGH

7: BETWEEN ALDE and BLYTH

Ancient city, modern power

LET'S START WITH A MYSTERY. The River Alde rises from several springs near Laxfield, goes under the A1152 at Snape, and nearly reaches Orford, its mouth at the time of the Norman Conquest. The Ore rises near Saxtead Green, flows through Framlingham and joins the Alde near Blaxhall. Then comes the Alde. But where the Alde finishes, the Ore picks up again, to pass Orford and enter the sea at Shingle Street.

There are two precedents. The Great Ouse changes its name to the Cam as it goes through Cambridge, and the Thames becomes the Isis at Oxford. But why should Saxmundham be on the Fromus? Shouldn't that flow through Framlingham?

The Blythe also rises near Laxfield, passes Halesworth, and reaches the sea near Southwold. The area between these streams is a region of small towns and past glories: Dunwich, once a capital city; Leiston, which had an ironworks; Saxmundham, a medieval market town; and Aldeburgh, which once built ships. Even Sizewell is at its peak as it will never have a third nuclear power station. Yet there is a bonus in past glories, as the present day is peaceful, a time oasis in a desert of turmoil.

ALDEBURGH

Aldeburgh is what its name infers, an *old borough*, more properly an *old fort*, referring to the Roman settlement now lost to the sea. So the river took its name from the town.

Salt. In 1327 were recorded the names of 33 townspeople who had assets worth 5s (25p); it was a sign of wealth rather than poverty, for the people were producing sea salt from pans south of town. By 1634 salt was so important that the corporation had to fight off an attempt from an outsider to be granted the monopoly on salt manufacture from Berwick to Southampton.

Salt was vital to the fishing industry, and here lay the real wealth of

Aldeburgh as the church register shows, with these family names in use locally: Carp, Crabbe, Pike, Sammon, Shrimp, Spratte, Turbette, Wale and Whiting.

Charter. Henry VIII granted the town its charter in 1529 after destroying Snape's Benedictine Monastery which had ruled the area. The town also had the right to send two Members to Parliament, which it did until the reforms of 1832. Edward VI helped all fishing communities in 1548 by banning the eating of meat on Fridays and Saturdays, with Wednesdays following in 1563. But soon the corporation was seeking more help, petitioning Elizabeth I to protect it from Dunkirk privateers.

Shipbuilding. For generations ships had been built at **Slaughden**, some vessels sailing against the Armada in 1588, but in Stuart times Slaughden was launching into the Alde the biggest ships in England. The decline was steady, and by 1830 the shipwrights were turning out 80-ton fishing smacks. In 1870 a local man drilled holes in his hull so he could bring live cod back from Iceland. The idea never worked. Thirty years later a storm wiped Slaughden from the map and boatbuilding was at an end.

Fishing. There were many reasons why fishing also declined. Dutch competition, erosion, the lengthening of Orford Beach, the digging of Lowestoft Harbour, the coal-fired trawler. Aldeburgh's fishing fleet is now confined to small boats which don't go far and which are hauled up on the beach.

Marquess of Salisbury. Early in the 19th cent the Marquess of Salisbury sought the newly-discovered pleasure of sea-bathing without the crowds that flocked to Brighton. His visit to Aldeburgh made the town a fashionable resort.

Railway. Tourism and fishing had a boost when the railway came. But it nearly never happened. The spur from Saxmundham to Leiston which opened on 1 June 1859 was to serve Garrett's ironworks only: Garrett was a director of the East Suffolk Railway. During laying, the line was granted permission to run on to Aldeburgh, which had its first train on 12 April 1860.

Thorpeness Halt opened on 29 July 1914 to serve that growing resort, but despite this the line made a profit for only a few years. Aldeburgh lost its freight service in November 1959 and the last passenger travelled in September 1966. The building of Sizewell nuclear power station gave the Leiston section a reprieve but the town's goods depot closed on 7 May 1984. Only the freight to and from Sizewell keeps the line open.

GEORGE CRABBE

Aldeburgh's most famous son is George Crabbe, born on Christmas Eve 1754 on the seaward side of the Moot Hall. Crabbe senior was the local saltmaster – tax collector – responsible for the sea salt refined here and at Slaughden. With two sons drowned, Crabbe was pleased when George opted for a land-based job, and became apprenticed to a surgeon in Woodbridge. After, he went to London for nine months of study, then came back home to set up his practise.

But this surgeon had a poet in him, trying to escape. In 1775, aged 20, Crabbe had his first verse, *Inebriety,* published in Ipswich. Drunk with success he headed to London to capture the literary world, but it eluded his grasp. In 1780 he managed *The Candidate,* but the next year he was back in Aldeburgh – as the local curate!

He was ordained in Norwich in 1781 and moved on to Belvoir Castle, Rutland, coming back to Beccles where he married his childhood sweetheart. He wasn't a happy priest either, for he lived in Aldeburgh, Lowestoft, Great Glemham, Rendham, London, Hastings, Bristol, Edinburgh, Frome, Stathern (Leics) and Muston (Leics). He was rector of Muston for 11 years yet was absent without leave for six of them! He dabbled again in surgery and when his wife died he moved on to Trowbridge where he died in 1832, aged 77.

Peter Grimes. His main achievements were *The Newspaper* in 1785 and *The Borough* in 1810, in which he created the character of Peter Grimes, the outcast:

> Thus by himself compelled to live each day,
> To wait for certain hours the tide's delay;
> At the same times the same dull views to see,
> The bounding marsh-bank and the blighted tree;
> The water only, when the tides were high,
> When low, the mud half-covered and half-dry;
> The sun-burnt tar that blisters on the planks,
> And bankside stakes in their uneven ranks;
> Heaps of entangled weeds that slowly float,
> As the tide rolls by the impeded boat.

His last work was *Tales of the Hall,* published in 1819 when he was living in London.

Benjamin Britten. Benjamin Britten took the character of Peter Grimes and turned him into a successful opera. Britten was born in Lowestoft in November 1913 and educated at Gresham's School, Holt and the Royal College of Music. He worked for the GPO film unit and was in the USA from 1939 to 1942. He founded the Aldeburgh Festival in 1948, with other musicians, and saw it become his life's work. He lived with fellow composer Peter Pears at Crag House, Crabbe St from 1947 to '57.

He became a Freeman of Lowestoft in 1953 and of Aldeburgh in 1962, and a member of honourary academies in Belgium, Germany,

Italy, Britain, Sweden and the USA. He died on 4 December 1976.

Writers. Aldeburgh, and Suffolk, attract writers and artists. Wilkie Collins (*The Moonstone*) was here in 1862; Old Fitz knew the town well; Thomas Carlyle stayed here, and Thomas Hardy had links with the town. More recently Laurens van der Post lived here; E.M. Forster (*A Passage to India*) was a regular visitor at Crag House; Ruth Rendell has connections; Kathleen Hale (*Orlando the Marmalade Cat*) came often; and Julia Lange of TV's *Listen With Mother* retired here.

Snooks. And don't forget Snooks, the dog remembered in the statue by the Moot Hall. His owners were doctors Robin and Nora Acheson who had a practice in town. Dr Nora wrote a smuggling story *Up The Steps*, set in the town.

ELIZABETH GARRETT ANDERSON

Aldeburgh's most famous daughter-by-adoption is Elizabeth Garrett Anderson, born in London in 1836. Her father Newson Garrett was the son of the man who founded Garrett's ironworks in Leiston, and was the man who bought a corn and coal warehouse at Snape and converted it into a malting house. He settled in Uplands house, now a hotel, opposite the church.

Elizabeth spent her childhood at Uplands but met an American woman who had qualified as a doctor and opened a dispensary in New York. Elizabeth decided to do the same in London.

But no college would admit her, purely because she was female. Eventually she found a loophole and began nursing in the Middlesex Hospital. She became Britain's first licensed apothecary in 1865, and opened her first dispensary the next year. A cholera outbreak led to the rapid opening of the second dispensary.

Paris. In 1865 Paris University opened its degree courses to women, and Elizabeth graduated in 1870, the first woman doctor from the Sorbonne. Within months she was Britain's first practising woman doctor, in east London, and became a member of the London School Board.

James Skelton Anderson. She met a senior medical administrator, James Anderson, who was also in shipping, and they married. But Elizabeth, now an ardent member of the Suffragettes, refused to lose her surname: she became Mrs Elizabeth Garrett Anderson. Skelton later co-founded the Orient Line which was later merged with the Peninsular Line to form today's P&O.

There was a tremendous demand for a hospital for women staffed by women, so in 1872 Elizabeth opened a small ward over her second dispensary. Two years later it became the New Hospital for Women in Marylebone Road, and Elizabeth was elected to the British Medical Association.

The Garrett Andersons retired to Aldeburgh in 1902 and by 1907

Skelton was mayor. He died in office, and Elizabeth agreed to serve out his term. Next year she was elected to the office in her own right, at 72 becoming Britain's first woman mayor. This remarkable woman died in December 1917, aged 81, and was remembered in the Elizabeth Garrett Anderson Hospital, London.

THE TOWN

Moot Hall. The most prominent building is the 16th-cent Moot Hall, built some distance from the sea but now standing on the beach, the town's most vulnerable property.

For many generations the first floor served as the council chamber and in more remote times as a magistrate's court as well. The open ground floor was a market place, but was bricked in when the market moved on. The town lost borough status in 1974 but retains its mayor, who still presides over council meetings on the first floor.

Museum. Outside of council hours, the entire hall is now the town museum (access via first floor door), open daily at limited hours, for

Aldeburgh's newest lifeboat in its new shed

a fee. You'll find a fascinating display of the town's history, including a whale's shoulder blade used as a sign on Slaughden's Three Mariners pub from 1550. There are Neolithic axe-heads, treasures from the Saxon ship-burial by Snape Church excavated in 1862, and many other relics of the past.

Trinity House. Before Trinity House was founded in 1514 to establish lighthouses. the townspeople burned barrels of tar on the church tower to help homecoming fishermen. Much later two towers were built on the sealine to search for ships needing pilots. Why two towers? Legend claims the lookouts were really watching for ships about to be wrecked, and the Up-towners and the Down-towners would race in open boats for the glory and riches of the salvage.

RNLI. The Royal National Lifeboat Institution put an end to the salvage gangs, but one of the towers was part of the RNLI station.

The first private lifeboat in the area was at Dunwich from 1826, but the RNLI opened its first station at Aldeburgh in 1851, and ran two stations until 1959. The last boat, *James Cable*, was parked on the beach ready for instant use, but the new boat, *Freddie Cooper*, is lauched from a trailer and is kept in a new shed. It has twin 285hp turbo-diesels with a range of 180 nautical miles at full speed, and has a crew of six. Most days the shed is open and you may inspect this marvellous craft at deck level.

To see how lifeboats have improved, look at the rudder of an old oarpowered boat standing outside the shed and remember that in 1928 the then number one boat had only oars and sails, and wasn't self-righting. The number two boat had a German name, *Edward Z. Dresden,* and in 1918 towed a downed seaplane back to Felixstowe.

Lifeboat disaster. 1899 is a year to remember in Aldeburgh. The lifeboat, named from the town, was an oared boat crewed by six men and on 7 December she was lost with all hands when answering a call. She had saved 152 lives in her 19 years on station before her own sinking. A brass memorial to the disaster is inside the church door.

Church. The nave and aisles of Ss Peter and Paul's Church form an enormous square which could easily hold the town's population, although not in the pews. Entry is from the car park (donations) through a door in the base of the tower. The original nave was Norman, enlarged immediately after the destriction of Snape Priory. Most of the stained glass was 19th cent, but a bomb in 1941 smashed 10 of the 13 but missed the east window, which has machine gun bullet holes in it. The **Benjamin Britten Window** was dedicated at the start of the 1980 Aldeburgh Festival and pictures the composer's three parables. The vestry has a bust of George Crabbe.

The church is normally open 0900-1900.

Martello tower. Slaughden's martello tower, or redoubt, is the northernmost in the chain which was built to defend England against Napoleon. The name and design come from a tower at Cape Mortella, Corsica, but this one is extra large and took 1,000,000 bricks to build. Although it's now on the edge of the beach, it has been restored and you may book it for a self-catering holiday: call the Landmark Trust on 01628.825925.

Cinema. Most towns as small as Aldeburgh would have lost their cinema years ago. This one threatened closure in 1970 but the public rallied round and 700 of them now pay around £12 a year to subsidise the picture palace. The auditorium was restored in 1994 for £30,000 by a sponsor-a-seat appeal at £50 a time. Among the sponsors were Libby Purves of TV (she lives nearby), Mstislav Rostropovich, John Gummer (then Minister of Agriculture) and Warner Brothers.

It's not just a cinema. There's a gallery for hire, a video library, and the **tourist information office,** open daily Easter-Oct, 01728.453637.

SNAPE and the Maltings.

Benjamin Britten, Peter Pears and Eric Crozier founded the **Aldeburgh Festival** in 1948, with the first season's operas staged in the church and jubilee hall. As the festival expanded it took in Orford, Framlingham and Blythburgh churches, and came to Snape in June 1967. At the end of the opening night two years later, the malthouse, converted to a theatre, burned down. Its replacement was a theatre looking like a malthouse, and was ready for the next season.

Snape is now the home of the Aldeburgh Festival every June, but the **Snape Maltings Riverside Centre** is a busy cultural centre open all year, with a selection of places to visit, including a gallery, art shop, tea room, bar, and several other shops. The *Plough and Sail* pub on the site also runs its own restaurant.

Several boats moor at the quay, offering cruises under sail or power to destinations downriver and out to sea. Call the Maltings Centre on 01728.688303 for details.

Snape village. Snape grew up at a crossroads near the head of navigation of the Alde River. An important man was buried in his longship here between 635 and 650, but the 1862 excavations ruined almost everything. The first church was built nearby, to be replaced in the 13th cent. This church was in ruins by the 15th cent and restoration was completed only in 1920. As Snape wasn't on a river it didn't have commercial clout.

Priory. Religious clout, yes. The priory was founded in 1155, soon after Nicholas Breakspear became the only English Pope. Henry VIII demolished it in 1524 as part of his campaign against the Papacy, and the only trace of it is in the name of Priory Farm.

THE NATIONAL TRUST
Dunwich Heath.

The National Trust owns Dunwich Heath, which is an important survival of the Suffolk Sandlings heathland, five miles from Orford Ness, the internationally important shingle spit south of Aldeburgh.

Dunwich Heath, one mile (1.6km) south of Dunwich Village, signposted from the A12, comprises 215 acres (87ha) of heathland and a mile (1.6km) of coastline. It is an excellent base for exploring the area on foot. There is a circular walk on the heath which links in to the Heritage Coast footpath, and there is also good access to the beach. The Coastguard Cottages house a tearoom, shop, holiday flats, and a first-floor observatory with telescope and binoculars.

There is a charge for parking at Dunwich Heath (free to National Trust members), where special events take place throughout the year including guided walks, fungi forays, summer holiday activities for children, and 'Pudding Experiences' in the tearoom. For further information call 01728.648505.

Pictures show the heath, and children pond-dipping on the heath.

See also page 80.

●

Orford Ness.

The National Trust bought five miles of Orford Ness from the Ministry of Defence in 1993, and opened to the public for the first time in June that year. Access is by boat from Orford Quay and is limited to Thurs, Fri, Sat, Apr-Oct. It is advisable to book crossings by calling Peter Weir at the Orford Ness Ferry on 01394.450057.

Access is limited by time and numbers because of the fragile nature of the shingle habitat and the condition of some of the large structures which survive from military occupation. The ness is an internationally important shingle spit which is home to rare plants, and a breeding site for several species of seabirds. The Royal Flying Corps first occupied the site in 1915, from which date until the Atomic Weapons Research Establishment left in the 1970s, the ness was used for secret military research.

See also page 59.

Coal, grain, malt. Ships brought coal up the Alde and exchanged it for grain at the head of navigation, where the main road (now the A1152) crossed the river. As Orford Beach made the journey less rewarding, the warehouses closed, to be bought up by Newson Garrett for conversion to a malt house.

●

EAST ANGLIAN TRANSPORT MUSEUM

As a museum under constant development, the Transport Museum is a prime example of what dedicated enthusiasts can achieve. The result is the only museum in the British Isles offering a complete historical transport experience with opportunities to view, and also to travel on some of the exhibits. There are no extra fares as these are covered by the admission fee.

The Woodland Tramway takes visitors along a cobbled street and then into woods, while other trolleybuses operate in an authentic 19th-cent townscape.

The narrow-gauge East Suffolk Light Railway runs from the authentic booking-office of Chapel Road Station to Woodside Halt, bringing to life a touch of railway history.

The collection of road vehicles is one of the most varied of any such museum, featuring some of the famous names in British industrial history: Armstrong-Whitworth; Thorneycroft; Ransomes, Sims & Jefferies; Garrett; Leyland, etc. There are steamrollers, cars, buses, vans, and even milk floats, and visitors are welcome to browse around the depots to appreciate the work that goes into conserving these vehicles.

A well-stocked bookshop caters for family tastes and the Terminus Tearooms café offers drinks and snacks. The museum is open summer weekends and peak season weekdays; for details call 01502.518459.

See also page 96.

●

Malt proved profitable for many years, prompting a spur railway 2.2km (1.4 miles) long from the main East Suffolk Railway to the maltings. There never was a station and horses were the only means of traction, but the line carried away up to 17,000 quarters (212 tons) of malt each year. When it closed on 7 March 1960 it was still using track laid in 1880. The maltings closed soon after, to await Benjamin Britten.

Sternfield. How good was life in the so-called 'good old days?' The *Ipswich Journal* reported on 25 March 1763: At the affizes held at Bury [St Edmunds] Yefterday, Marg. Beddingfield, Widow, and R. Ring, Hufbandman, were found guilty of the Murder of John Beddingfield, late of Sternfield, Farmer. The Woman was fentenced to be burnt, and the Man to be hanged and his Body anatomized.

And on 8 April: This Day Margery Beddingfield and Richard Ringe [sic] were drawn on a Sledge to the Place of Execution, where fhe was ftrangled and burnt, and he hanged.

Execution by fire as late as 1763? Ghastly! There is no recognisable headstone to any Beddingfield or Ring(e) in St Mary's churchyard.

LEISTON

Leiston has a ruined abbey and an ironworks museum, but the story behind both begins in the parish church.

St Margaret's Church. St Margaret of Antioch was martyred around 285-300. She became the patron saint of women in childbirth, and also of Leiston.

Sir Ranulf de Glanville, Chief Justiciar to Henry II, founded the **Abbey of the Premonstratensians** on Minsmere marshes in 1182, but in 1363 Robert de Ufford, Earl of Suffolk, rebuilt the abbey on its present site. It was to become the largest monastery in the county.

In 1536 **Leiston Abbey** had an income of £182 which brought it within the scope of Henry VIII's grand plan, and it was duly ruined, to something like its present state. Henry gave the ruins in 1537 to Charles Brandon, Duke of Suffolk, and the ousted abbot received a generous annuity of £20.

The church was not affected by the abbey's rise and fall, but a curious record from 1566 notes that Agnes Ward of Sizewell was lame and *could not come to the parish church of Leyston, so her said husband obtyned lycence to be married* in Sizewell chapel.

In the 17th cent **Richard Garrett** began working in iron in Woodbridge, but moved to Leiston in 1778. The business was mainly responsible for the population doubling in a century. And by this time Lady Rendlesham and her daughter the Hon Miss Sophia Thelluson were living in **Leiston Old Abbey**, a new building on the site of Ranulf's original.

As the hot-gospelling Rev John Calvert Blathwayt had come to town in 1837, the ladies saw need for a larger church. The original nave was a tunnel-like 39m (128ft) long by 6.2m (20ft) wide. After the ladies' fundraising the church was rebuilt in 1853 in Gothic Revival style for £2,500 with a wide nave and leaving only the tower and font from the original.

The design was controversial and Buckton Lamb, the architect, was reviled and died penniless, without even a memorial in the church. But Richard Garrett II, erstwhile deputy Lieutenant of Suffolk, has a grand plaque. Three of Garrett's stovepipe hats are preserved under glass in the town's Council Chamber.

And still the ironworks prospered. The town had 2,252 people in 1871, 3,259 in 1901, and 4,632 in 1921, and thereafter declined.

Leiston Abbey today. Miss Ellen Wrightson bought the abbey ruins in 1918, restored the Lady Chapel as a house of prayer and extended the Tudor farmhouse on the edge of the nave. When she died in 1946 the abbey and her house passed to the Diocese of St Edmundsbury and so to its present owner, English Heritage. It's open at any time with no fee.

The farmouse and restored barn are home to Pro Corda, the National Association of Young Chamber Music Players.

The Long Shop Museum. Richard Garrett Engineering closed in 1980 bringing economic disaster to the town, but in 1981 a museum arose from the long shop, probably the scene of Britain's first assembly-line manufacture. The museum is open daily Apr-Sep 1000-1600 for a fee. 01728.832189.

Garrett pioneered steam power in East Anglia, building traction engines, road rollers, and a wide assortment of unpowered machinery. Major exhibits include the only survivor of eight steam-driven tractors built in 1917, and a 4hp traction engine which uses 7kg (16lb) of coal and 55 litres (12 gallons) of water per mile.

USAAF Yoxford. There's also a section devoted to the `Yoxford boys' of the US Army Air Force 357th fighter group who operated from an airfield west of Leiston Abbey. Among the pilots who served here was Capt 'Chuck' Yeager who was the first man to fly supersonic, and live. The date? 14 October 1947, in the USA.

SIZEWELL

Sizewell is probably better known than anywhere else between Ipswich and Lowestoft, due to its magnesium-alloy Magnox gas-cooled nuclear power station A, and Britain's first pressurised water reactor, B. In 1995 the Government announced there would be no C.

The public was excluded from Sizewell A, but the PWR station welcomes visitors and has an information centre open daily, free. Call 01728.642139 for an update. Your appreciation will depend on your interest in pure science; you can play with a Geiger counter, learn that a ton of uranium produces as much energy as 20,000 tons of coal, that 70,000 tons of steel went into the construction, that the French-built reactor cost £10,000,000 and is cooled by 750 gallons of sea water per minute, and that the station can produce 1,200mw, enough to supply all East Anglia.

Footpath. The Suffolk Coastal footpath has a slight kink, but runs through the site. Sizewell hamlet survives, offering a large car park, café, pub and phone box. The dunes are of good sand but the beach is shingly.

THORPENESS and ALDRINGHAM

Aldringham is a small village on a crossroads. Look for the **Aldringham Craft Market** where a wide range of wares is available, usually including pottery, weaving, and articles in glass, leather and wood. The coffee shop sells home-made cakes. Open daily; 01728.830397.

Ogilvie family. The parish church is small, simple and poor, but its main feature is a small plaque to Fergus Mentieth Ogilvie of Barcaldine, Argyll, who died in 1918. So who was he? The father of Glencairn Stuart Ogilvie.

THORPENESS

Thorpeness never evolved. It was designed on a drawing board. G. S. Ogilvie bought the Sizewell estate in 1910, which included a fishing village called Thorpe. He set about creating a model village and a fashionable resort. He engaged labourers to dig a shallow lake, The Meare, by hand, naming its 20 islands from characters in *Peter Pan*, to please his friend J.M. Barrie. Barrie was indeed pleased, but the navvies were not: Ogilvie considered them unfit to walk the roads so they had to travel across the fields.

Ogilvie had a well dug, and installed a redundant windmill from Aldringham to pump the water into a tank atop a tower 26m (85ft) tall. He disguised the tank as a house, and so created **The House in The Clouds.** Don't be confused: what looks like the house was the tank; what look like supports for the tank, are the house.

A shell, aimed at a flying bomb in 1943, smashed the corner of the sectional tank, reducing capacity from 50,000 gallons to 30,000. The tank was dismantled in 1977 so the extra space has become an extention of the house. Nowadays the 5-bed 3-bath 2-recep house is available for letting for about £500 a week; call 0171.252.0743 for details.

The windmill no longer pumps, and is now the **visitor centre**, open May-Sep limited hours. During those hours you may climb to the fantail and have a good view across country.

Church. Ogilvie built St Mary's Church in 1936 and had it dedicated, not consecrated, so it's available to any denomination as well as social events.

The houses were originally built for summer occupation but after Ogilvie died in the 1970s, death duty forced their sale. They're now occupied year-round, so much insulation has been needed. The Ogilvie family still owns The Meare and the thatched barn, but the model village has certainly grown up.

SAXMUNDHAM

The quiet little town of Saxmundham was granted its market in 1272 and 40 years later it occupied a seven-acre (3ha) site. Most of the church's history is lost but the oldest bits were built around 1250 on a Saxon site, which helped give the town its name. The font has a carved woodwose – a tree spirit or green man – but the main feature is the chancel which 'weeps' to the left when seen from the altar. Some people claim this is sinister, but the more understanding of us know that it means Christ died for the impenitent thief as well as for the penitent.

The Bell Hotel, rebuilt in the 1840s, has character.

KELSALE-cum-CARLTON. The parishes merged generations ago, but Carlton Hall, which has Carlton Church in its grounds, was home to several men named Richard Garrett. Kelsale's half-timbered guildhall, built around 1495, is worth a look.

Splendid Ogilvie architecture at Thorpeness

77

THEBERTON, MIDDLETON, WESTLETON, MINSMERE

The trio of villages that circle Minsmere are all small. **Theberton**, twinned with Thebarton in Australia, was TV man David Frost's home in the 1980s. The beautifully-thatched Church of St Peter has a short Norman tower, and a Norman arch leading into the vestry.

Zeppelin. For years a World War I machine gun, captured at Gallipoli, stood by the church gate. It was given in recognition of the Victoria Cross awarded posthumously to a local man but in 1985 it went to the Royal Anglian Regiment for restoration. Part of a Zeppelin shot down here in 1917 used to hang in the south porch, but has now gone.

Eel's Foot Inn. Medieval priest John Neale caught the Devil in his boot, then took him to the coast and hurled him into the sea. Over the years Neale's boot has been corrupted to Eel's Foot, the name of the local inn.

Middleton. Holy Trinity Church once shared its yard with the church for Fordley, a village that decayed in the 16th cent. There's a Norman arch in the south porch and traces of a 15th-cent painting of St Christopher in the nave. discovered in 1908. The thatched Bell Inn and the water pump on the green, give the village a picture postcard image.

Westleton. Across the Minsmere River lies Westleton, where the tower of St Peter's Church partly collapsed in 1770, taking all eight bells. The number of collapsed towers in the area shows that no inspections and probably no maintenance was ever done. A World War II landmine dropped nearby, doing further damage, but one bell is rehung.

Witch's Stone. Students of architecture love to admire the Decorated style which has survived almost unaltered, but others come for the elusive Witch's Stone, a broken headstone by the chancel door. Leave your handkerchief here, run widdershins (anticlockwise) around the church three times and your hanky will disappear. Make it seven times and you'll hear the ghostly rattle of chains. Or is it the other way around?

Minsmere. The Royal Society for the Protection of Birds manages the reserve at Minsmere: there is no village of that name. A sandbank closed off the estuary of the Minsmere River 200 years ago and in 1890 the land was reclaimed. It was flooded again in 1940 as coastal defence, and by 1945 it was a perfect habitat for wading birds. The RSPB leased the site in 1949 from Stuart Ogilvie of Thorpeness and so began one of the most important reserves in eastern England. The marsh covers 460 acres (185ha) and the woodland another 600 acres (240ha).

More than 100 species of bird have been seen here, the notable ones being the marsh harrier, bittern and avocet. Access is from

Westleton and the reserve is open daily except Tues and Christmas, 0900-1700 or dusk; fee. The Suffolk Coastal Path runs along the fore-shore with access to free hides.

DUNWICH

In ancient times the coast was a mile or more further out to sea, and the Dunwich River had a large harbour. The Romans had a settlement here, called **Dumnocaister**. Felix, who landed at Babingley near King's Lynn, made the little town the seat of his bishopric of the East Angles; he died in 647. The Vikings saw an enticing estuary and called in **Dunevik,** and King Guthrum, who became the first Christian Viking in these parts, chose the town as the capital of the Danelaw, an area stretching from The Wash to Northampton to Colchester. Guthrum died in the 9th cent.

But the erosion never ceased. Year by year the eastern part of the city was washed away, and the harbour gradually filled.

At the Domesday survey the population was around 3,000 and rising. Kings John, Henry III and Edward I relied on the town of Dunwich to supply their warships, and it was John who gave the charter, with rights over all east coast wrecks, in return for 5,000 eels a year. But the sea never relented, and a storm of 1328 blocked the harbour mouth, sealing the town's fate.

We know nothing of the Roman or early medieval street plan, and we can only guess at the Tudor layout, but we do know that the first of Dunwich's nine churches was lost in 1320, with two more in the next 20 years. All have now gone – but a tiny part of the last church, abandoned in the 1750s, was saved in 1923 and has been rebuilt beside the newish Church of St James, finished in 1832. Nearby are the ruins of St James's leper colony.

Legend claims that the bells of those nine churches can be heard ringing on the sea bed during storms – but if any bells were lost they'll be in Orford Ness by now.

Downing. Sir George Downing bought property in the town and so qualified to become its MP – in truth one of two MPs, for this was another rotten borough. He was unpopular and never won an election by fair means; on one occasion he got all his tenants into debt and threatened them with eviction if they didn't vote for him. Sir George left money to finance the building of Downing College in Cambridge and another member of the family gave some property in Downing Street, London, to the Prime Minister of the day. It was the Reform Act of 1832 which abolished the rotten boroughs, and the last MP of Dunwich was Frederick Barn, lord of the manor, who died in 1886.

Ship and Flora. Thousands of visitors come to Dunwich each year, with a choice of two places to eat. The Flora Tea Rooms by the vast car park are named from the barge *Flora* which sank here in 1888; her timbers were used in the building which burned down in 1988. The present building opened in 1989.

The Ship is allegedly one of the first inns in England to be licensed, and it has stood here since Tudor times as the harbour was just across the road. Another legend claims that a tunnel runs from the Ship's cellars to Greyfriars Priory. We shall learn the truth when the sea claims the priory.

Museum. Dunwich has a splendid little museum in St James's St – the *only* street – open daily May-Sep and limited times in spring and autumn: 01728.73358 for details. The main exhibit is a relief model of Dunwich in early Medieval times, showing what has been lost to the cruel sea.

DUNWICH HEATH. See page 72 for this National Trust property. Cliff House caravan and chalet park, on the road down to the heath, is a beautifully scenic place to stay.

Toby's Walks. Where the Walberswick Road meets the A12 south of Blythburgh is the picnic spot known as Toby's Walks. Tobias Gill was a black drummer in the Dragoons, and one night in 1750 when he was drunk he walked out of his quarters in Blythburgh and met a Walberswick serving maid, Anna Blackmore, whom he allegedly raped and murdered; he was found sleeping by her body. Convicted at Ipswich, he was chained hand and foot and hanged at the crossroads. As he was denied a Christian burial, his ghost haunts the heath sitting on a black hearse drawn by four black horses.

Slaughden's Redoubt is the most northerly Martello Tower in England

80

BLYTHBURGH

On a Sunday morning in August 1577 a terrible storm damaged the tower of Blythburgh Church, destroying the steeple, killing three of the congregation and shocking others. All the victims wore burn marks consistent with lightning strike, but witnesses claim it was a visit by **Black Shuck** the ghostly dog who haunts East Anglia. The dog then flew on to Bungay and killed two people in the church there. If you doubt the story, look at the plaque on a lamp standard near Bungay's Butter Cross.

Of course, other knowalls thought it was the Devil himself: who else would leave such scratches on the door?

Xestobium refovillosum. In the 1970s Holy Trinity Church was attacked again, by creatures whose mating call is an ominous clicking which earns them the name of death watch beetle. The church is enormous for such a tiny village; the nave is 38.6m (127ft) long and you could probably squeeze half the village's pre-1950s houses inside it: you could certainly hold all the people thirty times over. No wonder it's called the Cathedral of the Marshes.

A church was here from 620, before Butwulf founded Iken. The present tower was built around 1330 although Black Shuck took its steeple. The existing nave is mostly 15th cent, taking 80 years to build. William Dowsing called in 1644, ordered the churchwardens to strip out all the brasses, after which he fired lead shot into all the timberwork, fixed tethering rings to the columns, and stabled his horses inside.

Two centuries later an angel's wing fell from the roof, the last victim of Dowsing's shot, but by then the church was long derelict and the windows were bricked up. In the 1870s the returning congregation sat under umbrellas, and the church officially reopened in 1884.

Jack-o'-the-Clock. Two fittings are of interest. A Jack-o'-the-Clock similar to the one in Southwold (look closely and you'll see it's not a Jill), and an alms box of 1473. It's often called a Peter's Pence box, as from 750 the church began sending money to Rome regardless of the poverty at home. After the break with Catholicism all alms stayed at home, which made more sense.

Bustling town. Edward the Confessor held lands here in 1042, and the village is mentioned in Domesday. Henry I gave church money to the abbot of St Osyth, near Clacton, who founded a priory here at Blythburgh, but only a few stones remain. Henry IV gave the priory licence to rebuilt Holy Trinity and, as the town was bustling, the abbot built this enormous nave. Bustling? Blythburgh had two charter fairs, a Mint, a jail, and plenty of river traffic.

But the end was nigh. As Dunwich's trade collapsed, so did Blythburgh's. The river Blyth entered the sea through Dunwich Harbour, which was blocked by that storm of 1328. The river carved its own new exit to the sea nearer Walberswich, but Blythburgh's trade was mortally wounded. In 1478 records claim the town's income was *16d and no more*. It took more than a century for the river to be canalised to its present mouth, and that was far too late. The town was dead.

Haunted house. And so was the woman in the white dress. She had lived at **Westwood Lodge** south of the road to Walberswick, but she kept coming back in ghostly form. Even in 1972 policemen spent a night in the empty house hoping to apprehend her. She sprung their traps and chilled the air, but escaped. The lodge was the family seat of the Blois family (call it *bloyz*) and was built with narrow passages in the outer walls, so servants could move without disturbing the gentry. After being empty for many years the lodge is again occupied.

WALBERSWICK

Waldbert, a Saxon, built a small community on a *vik* or inlet which was to become the Blyth estuary in 1590, when Southwold and Walberswick men cut the new channel. But Waldbertsvik had long become the modern Walberswick, pronounced *Worbelzwik*.

The town was granted charters in 1262, 1483, 1485, 1553, 1558 and 1625, mostly to exempt tradesmen and merchants from tolls, with the result that Walberswick handled large quantities of timber, coal, fish, grain and salt. In 1451 the port had 13 ships trading with Iceland and Norway, and records of 1597 show that 2d (1p) duty was paid on every cargo of cheese, the money going to the churchwardens.

Two churches. Blythburgh Church controlled Walberswick's two churches, the older being demolished in 1473, leaving St Andrew's on its present site.

The tower of St Andrew's had been planned in 1426 and its builders, working in summer only, were to receive each year *40 scheelyngs of laughful money of Inglond, and a cade full of Herrynge.*

Around 1480 the nave was demolished and a much larger one built onto the 27m (90ft) tower, completed in 1493. The church lost its tithes – its income of 10% of local wealth – when Henry VIII demolished the nation's abbeys. Most of this money had been spent in the town, its loss beginning the economic decline. In 1585 the churchwardens were obliged to sell the great bell, weighing 774kg (1,707lb, 15cwt) for £26 8s 9d (44p) and in 1586 a fire destroyed part of the town reducing it to 54 families.. More fires in 1633, 1683 and 1749 were to reduce Walberswick to 20 houses and 100 people.

The result was obvious. The church had received no income for generations and the population had been much reduced. In 1695 the nave was dismantled just enough to yield masonry to build a much smaller one 19.5m (64ft) long within the original. Three bells, roof

St Andrew's, Walberswick, is a church within a church.

lead, and timber were sold for £303 1s 11d (10p) while the new nave cost £291.8s 9d (44p), giving a small profit.

Come to Walberswick today and you can see a church within a church, and marvel how Blythburgh and Walberswick could ever have afforded their enormous houses of God.

HALESWORTH

Sir Joseph Dalton Hooker, born at Halesworth in 1817, went on Ross's Antarctic expedition in 1839-40, then in 1848 he led a plant hunt to northern India. Seven years later he was assistant director of **Kew Gardens**, founded the *genera plantarum* there in 1862 and took full control of the gardens when its director died. The director was none other than his father, Hilliam Jackson Hooker. The Hooker family home, Brewery House, has survived, but its garden has not.

The small town was granted a markt in 1222 and the Blyth River was made navigable for barges in 1756.

Opposite the church is the Halesworth Gallery, May-Sep, daily, and the Halesworth Museum, May-Sep certain days. The museum concentrates on local geology, rural life, and the Halesworth witchcraft trials of 1645.

THE SOUTHWOLD RAILWAY

The East Suffolk Railway was born in 1854 from the merger of smaller lines, and built the track from Lowestoft down to Woodbridge.

From here the Eastern Counties Railway took it to Ipswich, the whole stretch opening in 1859. Both companies undertook the spur lines to Leiston, Snape and Framlingham, but nobody wanted to build a line to Southwold.

Eventually enough people were persuaded to form a company, but the 14.1km (8.75 miles) of the Southwold Railway would be on a 914cm (3ft) gauge, slightly narrower than the Great Eastern Railway main line, formed in 1862 from the ESR, the ECR and others. Despite this saving in outlay the construction costs were £8,504 per mile. The company was incorporated in 1876 and the line opened on 24 September 1879, running from Halesworth through Wenhaston, passing Blythburgh Church and the White Hart, going north of Walberswick and crossing the Blyth before running into Southwold. You can dismiss the legend that the rolling stock came from the Woosung Railway in China.

The GER offered to buy the line in 1893 but the directors of the SR weren't interested. The SR had to rebuild the Blyth swing bridge in 1907 to take the proposed standard gauge track, and prospects looked good as, by 1908, there were more than 300 herring drifters based at Southwold and using the SR to move their catches to market. The tourist traffic was growing, too, for in 1910 the SR carried 104,197 passengers as well as 12,824 tons of freight, mostly fish, coal, grain and milk.

Decline begins. Army camps replaced some of the traffic lost during World War I, but in 1918 the decline began, with the company showing its first loss in 1926, although it was just £4.

In 1928 Southwold Corporation allowed the dreaded motor omnibus into town. That was the year when buses were allowed to travel at 20mph (32kph), but the railway was permanently limited to 16mph (25kph). The London and North Eastern Railway, successor to the GER, offered to buy the Southwold Railway in 1923 but once again the directors refused to sell. A grave error: when they begged the LNER to buy in 1929, they were turned down. The SR closed on 11 April 1929, its track and rolling stock abandoned until 1941 when they were sold for scrap.

The Blyth bridge has been rebuilt as a footbridge, the lowest crossing point of the river, but there is a ferry further downstream.

8: BETWEEN BLYTH and WAVENEY

Fish and otters

SOUTHWOLD AND LOWESTOFT guard each end of this stretch of coast, while the historic towns of Bungay and Beccles lie on the south bank of the pleasant Waveney. It is an area of quiet countryside, with major industry confined to Lowestoft where you will find Britain's easternmost extremity, approached via Gasworks Road.

SOUTHWOLD

Southwold is a quiet and pleasant town, its character coming from its houses, mostly built after the disastrous fire of 1659. In the rebuilding, seven areas were left open – the town's 'greens' – as future firebreaks, although some historians claim the greens had always been there.

Lighthouse. The town is characterised by a dazzling white lighthouse which first shone in 1890 and is still in operation, though not open to the public.

Battle of Sole Bay. The Sole Bay Inn near the lighthouse recalls Southwold's greatest claim to fame as well as an enigma. Few reference books have ever heard of the Battle of Sole Bay, in which the combined English and French fleets fought the Dutch fleet in 1672 in Sole Bay. Few maps have ever marked it, the OS Pathfinder TH 47/57 being an exception. It's a very shallow indent north of the town.

So here's the story of the unknown battle in the unknown location, with variations in brackets.

England and France provoked the United Provinces, today's Netherlands and Wallonia, into the **Third Anglo-Dutch War**. England wanted to curtail the growing Dutch mercantile threat, and France saw it as a means of curtailing Spain, which still held interests in Holland.

The Dutch were trying to avoid a French victory on land but they, and the English, suspected Louis XIV had ordered his vice-admiral the Compte d'Estrées to go easy on the French amateur sailors. The

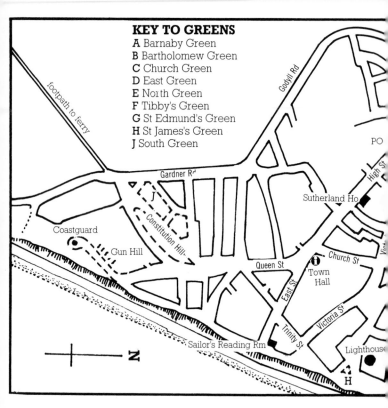

KEY TO GREENS

A Barnaby Green
B Bartholomew Green
C Church Green
D East Green
E North Green
F Tibby's Green
G St Edmund's Green
H St James's Green
J South Green

Dutch commander, Admiral Michiel de Ruyter (no – Admiral Banckers), who had attacked Landguard Fort and whose descendant invented Reuter's Press Agency, was not surprised to meet an Anglo-French fleet off Zeeland. He held his ground, and the Allies retreated – to Sole Bay.

Why there? Because James, Duke of York, Lord High Admiral, had made his headquarters in **Sutherland House**, which had missed the great fire. And so, on the morn of 28 May 1672, a French lookout saw the 91 (or 75) Dutch ships bearing down from the east-nor'-east in battle formation, with fireships in the vanguard and the wind dead astern.

Action was needed – fast. The English had men in Southwold getting water; the French were in Aldeburgh doing the same. And their ships were on a lee shore. The 101 (or 98) Allied ships hauled

York Rd

Police

Station Rd

A

E   Library

Museum

F

B

St Edmunds
Ch

Adnam's Brewery

C   G

Summer Theatre

D   Cumberland   Rd

Stradbroke Rd

Marlborough Rd

Buss Creek

boating Lakes

model yachts

SOUTHWOLD

anchors or cut cables and sailed, the 33 French going south-east, exchanging long-range gunfire with the Dutch and thereafter *hors de combat.*

The English, outnumbered three to two, sailed north and engaged the Dutch, losing four ships to the Dutch three ('heavy losses on both sides'). The battle continued until dusk, when the Dutch pulled away (or until the English received reinforcements).

●

THE OTTER TRUST

The Otter Trust is a registered public charity founded in 1972 by naturalist Philip Wayre and his wife Jeanne. The main aims are to promote the conservation of otters throughout the world, with particular emphasis on the British Otter. Its headquarters are in the Waveney Valley at Earsham where visitors can see the world's largest collection of otters including more than twenty enclosures devoted to breeding the British Otter.

The trust is the only organisation in the world breeding the British Otter regularly in captivity and in sufficient numbers to ensure a surplus of young animals for reintroduction into the wild every year, in order to prevent the animals' extinction in lowland England.

Visitors to Earsham can also see the playful Asian Short-clawed Otter, the smallest in the world. In addition there are three lakes with a great collection of European waterfowl, including full-winged flocks of wild geese and swans which fly freely across the marshes. There are attractive riverside walks where the diminutive Muntjac Deer can be seen at liberty in the small copse near the Trout Lake. At Earsham there is an attractive tearoom and gift shop as well as an Interpretive Centre.

Open daily Good Friday or 1 Apr to 31 Oct, 1030-1800; feeding times 1200, 1530.

Picture: a close view of an inquisitive otter.

See also page 98.

●

Sandwich. Edward Montagu, first Earl of Sandwich, was an early victim, his body being washed ashore near Harwich. He was great-grandfather to the gambler who couldn't spare time to eat, so put meat between chunks of bread and invented the sandwich.

Or maybe the battle didn't happen here at all? A letter datelined *Landguard Fort, May 28th '72, Tuesday evening 8 a clock* claims *I am but just come from Aldborow...where I found the Fleetes ingaged...*

The Dutch had a breathing space after Sole Bay, but ultimately Southwold's Duke of York, now crowned James II, handed over the throne to William III – William of Orange.

Care for a cruise from Snape Maltings?

Memorial to the lifeboatmen lost at Aldeburgh

SOUTHWOLD: the early years

In Saxon times, Southwold was a few huts on an island where fishermen dried their nets; the settlement was two miles away at Reydon. Domesday mentions the 25,000 herring that the community had to send each year to St Edmund's Abbey at Bury, which owned the manorial rights, although Jocelin de Brakelond was the lord in residence.

First church. John de Grey, Bishop of Norwich, had papal permission in 1202 to build a chapel on the island; it was, naturally, dedicated to St Edmund. It survived 200 years but nothing was known of it until its foundations were found in 1758 under the chancel of today's proud **St Edmund's Church.** This was begun around 1413, the year Henry V became king, but the swan and ermine of Henry IV are carved in a window mullion as Henry IV, like Edward IV, was lord of the Manor of Southwold. The church was probably completed in 1482, and Henry VII granted the town its charter in 1489.

Target practice. The Saxon king, Edmund, was slain by Danes in 870, probably at Shottisham, possibly at Hoxne. He was tied to a tree and whipped – no, he was used for target practice by archers. The east window and the Tennyson memorial window in the church both show Edmund, king, saint and martyr, with arrows about to hit.

By the way, the processional cross near the east window, came from the family of Emperor Haile Selassie of Ethiopia – and that's true.

William Dowsing destroyed the original font cover, among many other acts of desecration, but the 1936 replacement is 7.3m (24ft) tall, the highest in the country.

Southwold Jack. Southwold Jack is a doll-sized Wars of the Roses soldier fixed to the wall. Pull the cord hanging from his coat, and he strikes a bell with the hammer in his right hand, much as, ages ago a clock ordained him to strike the time. Shakespeare wrote in *Richard II:* "I stand fooling here like Jack o' the Clock."

Sutherland House. Few medieval buildings survived Southwold's fire, but the Duke of York's base in the Battle of Sole bay, is one which did. Now a smart restaurant, the original 16th-cent plaster ceilings are well worth seeing. The building was originally named from John Cammel, a local merchant who lived here in 1606, but Matthew Wren, brother of architect Sir Christopher, was here during the battle, and wrote his own report to Whitehall.

Gun Hill. Southwold had no defences before 1569 when the Earl of Warwick gave it eight cannon on condition the town supplied the powder, which it didn't. The burghers were again ordered to comply in 1580, but they didn't. Then in 1587 with the Armada threat looming, a survey of the town found it *weak but strongly situated* and sent eight guns for the north and others for the south. After the Armada threat receded, the guns rusted.

In January 1746 the town received six 18lb- Elizabethan cannon from Ordnance stores in Woolwich, reputedly captured at the Battle of Culloden – but they weren't – with 40 rounds for each, on the usual conditions. The corporation set up a battery on Gun Hill and in 1810 defied a suggestion that the guns be sent to Great Yarmouth. The cannon are still there today, but nobody has ever supplied any powder.

Museums. The **Southwold Museum**, housed in a Dutch-style cottage in Victoria Street since 1932, is open Easter-Sep daily, 1430-1630. Its exhibits are of local interest, including the railway and the Sole Bay battle. The **RNLI Museum** in the old Coastguard lookout on Gun Hill, is open on request to Mr Goldsmith, 01502.722422. The **Sailors' Reading Room** on East Cliff has books and exhibits of nautical interest.

Adnam's Brewery. The Sole Bay Brewery is known to have been in existence in 1641, probably behind the Swan Hotel. In 1872 it was still tucked in a corner of the hotel yard when the Adnams family bought it and began expansion. Soon they were buying up the competition and winning awards at home and abroad.

Adnams owns 70 pubs and hotels, including the Swan, and in 1970 it reintroduced horse-drawn drays for local deliveries. Among its pubs are the **Lord Nelson,** from whose dormer windows messages were flashed to smugglers at sea; the **Sole Bay Inn,** and the **Harbour Inn,** where landlord, customers and pets were marooned for a day in

Bungay Castle; the remains of the round towers built by the Bigod family

90

the 1953 floods. The **Southwold Arms** existed before 1803, the **Red Lion** was here in 1768 under a different name, and the **King's Head** was licensed in 1836.

Blyford. Adnams also owns the **Queen's Head** at Blyford, a well-known smuggling house from where the contraband was rushed across the road to All Saints' Church in time of danger. The church, by the way, has a Norman doorway.

NORTH OF SOUTHWOLD

Covehithe. The parish of Covehithe never had more than 300 people, yet St Andrew's Church was as big as a cathedral. Why? Because William Yarmouth, appointed priest in 1459, had the money to build it. At the time Covehithe was dependent on the priory of Wangford which was a satellite of Thetford Priory which was subordinate to the Benedictine Abbey of Cluny, France.

It was in 1672 that Covehithe realised it couldn't support its massive church, and it demolished Yarmouth's edifice to use the materials for a tiny church, still in use although its tower is redundant.

Coastal erosion. The lane east of Covehithe disappears over the cliff, which is cutting into the land at up to 3m (10ft) a year. In 1990 the news media focused on a couple who had bought an expensive house at **Easton Bavents** and had to abandon it a year later due to erosion.

Father Christmas. St Nicholas's Church at **Wrentham** tells the story of Nicholas, patron saint of Russia and lesser lands, cities, and provinces, of sailors, travellers, merchants, children, pawnbrokers, and anybody facing sudden danger. Saint Nick was born in today's Turkey and buried in Italy.

Henstead. A mile west of the A12, beyond Toad Row, is Henstead. St Mary's thatched church has a Norman doorway and also serves **Hulver Street,** a mile west, where holly was grown in the 13th cent.

KESSINGLAND

Stone Age man lived at Kessingland, when the sea was miles away. By the time the Vikings arrived they could sail up to **Frostenden,** and Kessingland was a major port, second only to Dunwich. The Norman lords demanded 22,000 herring a year from the 8,000 people, but Lowestoft was too insignificant to give anything.

It was the same old story. The sea silted up the estuary and the Great Plague killed many of the people. A lighthouse was built in 1850 but survived little more than 50 years; the RNLI put a lifeboat here in 1869 and withdrew it in 1936. And coastguard stations have come and gone.

Rider Haggard. The author of *She* and *King Solomon's Mines* bought a former coastguard station here for his house. He called it

Southwold's dazzling white lighthouse

Kessingland Grange and named each room from a famous admiral. The house has gone, but Rider Haggard Lane leads to the site.

Suffolk Wildlife Park. The Le Grys family bought the wildlife and rare breeds park in 1985 and have expanded it greatly. On 100 acres (40ha) you'll meet tiger, lynx, emus, camels, beavers, and many others. There's the four-horn loghtan sheep from the Isle of Man, and chimpanzees from *Gorillas In The Mist*.

LOWESTOFT

The Anglo-Saxons had a small fishing community where Lowestoft now stands, but it was too small to mention in Domesday. The fishing industry began expanding in the 13th cent as Kessingland's harbour began silting – but there was no harbour at all at Lowestoft. The size of **St Margaret's Church** of the 14th cent, infers it served a large village, as Beccles was the market town. Plague struck in 1349, killing 90% of the people, then it hit again in 1547, And in 1605 fire destroyed much of the town.

Lowestoft Harbour. As the Waveney silted, Oulton Broad became a lagoon, Lake Lothing, taking its name from Lovingland or Lozingland island, on which the small town stood. The name originated with Herbert de Losinga, first Bishop of Norwich.

Men cut through the sandspit, linking Lothing with the sea in May 1831, and so creating Lowestoft Harbour. But the wooden lock gate floated away on the first high tide.

Swing bridge. A bridge was needed over the harbour access. The second attempt, a single-span swing bridge which took 58 seconds to open, came into use in 1897, and was used 6,500 times annually in its first years. In 1970 it jammed in the open postion for boats and for six weeks split the town. The present double-bascule lift bridge came in 1972.

Railway. Let's go back to 1845 when Samuel Morton Peto, Lord of the Manor and owner of Somerleyton Hall, received permission to create the Lowestoft Railway & Harbour Company. By the next year the North Trawl Basin was dug, and in 1850 the South Basin was in business. Peto's railway had already linked with Norwich three years earlier, and steam packet boats were sailing regularly to Rotterdam, Hamburg and even St Petersburg. The Waveney Dock opened in 1883 and the Hamilton Dock in 1903, and Lowestoft was complete.

Boom times were here. In 1909 somebody calculated that Lowestoft and Great Yarmouth together landed 1,044,001,200 herring, and the GER moved most of them, sending up to 40 wagons every hour to London. But in 1916 the London and North Eastern Railway took over the GER and concentrated its efforts on Grimsby and Hull. Lowestoft's peak times were over.

War. Lowestoft was the first town to be bombed by the Germans in World War I – from a Zeppelin. After the war it was realised that fish stocks were low, and they have never been allowed to recover. Today Lowestoft has pensioned off almost all its trawlers and relies on serving the North Sea gas rigs – but stocks of gas will also run out one day.

LOWESTOFT TODAY

St Margaret's Church. The bronze plaque by the west window remembers Robert Browne, Snr and Jnr, who were organists for 94 years. Mr Browne Snr, whose father started the Lowestoft china factory, began playing at 14.

Christ Church on Lowestoft Ness proclaims itself as the most easterly church in the British Isles, but the weathercock on St Margaret's catches the morning sun before anywhere else in Britain – but only on the equinoxes. It is a great shame that the ness is dominated by an industrial sprawl.

Old Town. The old town, north of the bascule bridge, has a busy shopping centre on higher ground, with access to the shore by steep alleys or steps, known as *scores.* North of the lighthouse, Cart Score and Ravine Score lead down to the **Lowestoft and Suffolk Maritime Museum** in a fisherman's flint-built cottage. Nearby is the **Royal Naval Patrol Service Museum**. The **Lowestoft Museum** is in Oulton Broad.

Britten and Conrad. Benjamin Britten was born here in 1913. Teodor Josef Konrad Korzeniowski was born in Poland in 1857 but changed his name to Joseph Conrad when he jumped ship in Lowestoft. The harbourmaster taught Conrad the basics of English, from where he progressed to become a well-known novelist, his main work being *Lord Jim,* published in 1900. He was buried at Canterbury in 1924.

Traffic. In high summer traffic is a major problem in town with queues up to a mile long on each side of the harbour. The only bypass, Oulton Broad, is little better.

OULTON BROAD

Oulton Broad is devoted purely to pleasure. You can get self-drive boat hire, go swimming, play tennis, and many other sports. On Thursday evenings, Easter-Sep, there is power-boat racing for which the broad is famous.

George Borrow lived in the now-demolished Oulton Cottage and wrote *Lavengro* in the summerhouse. Although he died in 1881 some people claim his ghost still walks the grounds.

Samuel Morton Peto, once England's largest employer of labour, built Somerleyton village

NORTH OF LOWESTOFT

Gunton. China clay was found at Gunton Hall in 1756 and the following year Robert Browne, father of the first organist, led a consortium which went into business producing quality as well as cheap porcelain. Production ceased in 1802 and the factory was destroyed in World War Two.

Billy Butlin came here in the 1930s and started the mass-market holiday, which now dominates the village with Warner Holidays the market leader. Nearby is **Pleasurewood Hills** and the Crinkley Bottom theme park, with the course of the old **Norfolk and Suffolk Joint Railway** running through the site. And even closer is the only **naturist beach** in East Anglia.

Corton. Corton was in Suffolk until 1974, but it's still the birthplace of Jeremiah James Colman, the founder of the mustard empire. Colman's friend, William Gladstone, Prime Minister from 1868, gave the clock which is in the village hall.

Blundestone. The narrowest and tallest Saxon round tower in England is at this village, which Charles Dickens called *Blunderstone*, the birthplace of David Copperfield. The hall, built in 1785, is now a maximum-security prison.

SOMERLEYTON HALL

Samuel Morton Peto bought Somerleyton Hall and its 4,500-acre estate in 1843 and threw himself into the life of the landed gentry.

95

Born in Woking, he inherited wealth and a building business. He built the Reform Club and Nelson's Column, then turned to railways. After laying the line into Lowestoft he laid more in Algeria, Argentina, Canada, Denmark and Russia, and also became the largest employer of labour in Britain. He rebuilt Somerleyton Hall as well as the entire village of Somerleyton. He was Liberal MP for Norwich and elsewhere, a leading Baptist, and a public benefactor.

Somerleyton Hall today is a palace. The banqueting room has a ceiling 8.5m (28ft) high, the yew-hedge maze is among the best in Britain, and the 18.5cm (7.25in) gauge miniature railway runs for 450m. The hall is open Easter-Sep at select times: call 01502.730224 for details.

Crossley Carpets. Peto's company went broke in 1863, forcing the sale of the hall. The new owner was Sir Francis Crossley, one of three brothers who invented the steam-powered loom in 1851, enabling them to mass-produce carpets. Francis became a baron and his great-grandson is the present Lord Somerleyton, owner of the estate which includes Fritton Lake.

Fritton Lake Country Park. The park, in Norfolk since 1974, is built for family amusement, including golf, heavy horses, falconry, children's farm and boating. Open daily Apr-Sep.

EAST ANGLIAN TRANSPORT MUSEUM

A group of enthusiasts started the Transport Museum at Carlton Colville in 1965 with a few old vehicles. The first tramcar was operating in 1970 and has been joined by others, running on their own railway. There's also the only surviving piece of the Southwold Railway track and rolling stock.

See page 73 for more details.

BECCLES

Beccles is a small market town whose name has been carried around the world in books *printed by Wm Clowes, Beccles*. The printing works is hidden away in the town centre backstreets where it has been for more than a century.

The Saxons settled here, the Vikings called by, and Domesday recalls the market was jointly owned by William I and the Abbot of Bury St Edmunds – and the town had to send 60,000 herring each year to the abbot.

A chapel beside the market place had the fisherman St Peter as patron. Henry VIII seized it at the dissolution of the monasteries and gave it to William Rede who incorporated it into his house. It's still there, in what is now St Peter's Guest House.

The Saxon church has gone. The present Church of St Michael is

14th cent but its freestanding tower is 16th cent. Freestanding towers are rare in East Anglia, but as this one weighs around 3,000 tons, it would have slid into the river if it had been built in the normal place. The church has another oddity in its 'green man' or 'wodewose'. The green man, who has given his name to many pubs, was a tree spirit, the origin of the surviving custom of dancing around the maypole, and the source of the surname Wodehouse.

Roos Hall. Roos Hall missed the fire of November 1586. Thomas Colby had completed it in 1583 in Dutch style, remembering the wool trade between here and the Low Countries. Queen Elizabeth I stayed here in 1584 when she presented the town with its charter. Colby sold the hall to the Suckling family which was later to produce Catharine Suckling, mother of Horatio Nelson. Viewing of the hall is through the tourist office on the quay: 01502.713196.

Other Beccles houses. The former Quaker meeting house is now the **Beccles Museum** open Apr-Oct. William Clowes has its **Printing Museum** open daily Jul-Aug, holding some wonders from the world of words.

The King's Head Hotel began life as a coaching inn, but Oswold House on Northgate was the retirement home of Gen. Sir Claude Auchinleck, Commander-in-Chief Middle East until 1942.

GELDESTON. Geldeston Lock marks the head of the tidewater on the Waveney. The rights to use the canalised Waveney from here, were in private hands, and their 19th cent owner Mathias Kerrison made almost a million pounds from the trade.

BARSHAM. Barsham's Church of the Most Holy Trinity has a Saxon round tower 10m (33ft) tall topped by 7m (22ft) of Norman masonry. In 1912 the five bells were rung for 2 hours 40 minutes – not bad for a tower whose base was 900 years old!

BUNGAY

Bungay, too, has had its name carried worldwide by a book printer – Richard Clay, who started business in 1876. The town snuggles between a great loop in The Waveney River, giving it protection in medieval times, and earlier. And that is why Hugh Bigod, first Earl of Norfolk, began his castle here in 1164 or '65 – see Framlinghham and Orford.

Castle. The base of the walls of the keep was 5.5m (18ft) thick, the strongest yet built in England, and rising to 27m (90ft) by 1174. When King Henry decided the castle had to be destroyed, sappers began undermining one corner. Bigod capitulated and was allowed to hold onto the castle – but the sappers' cave is still there today.

When Bigod was killed in the Crusades, the castle began to decay but a Roger Bigod saved it in 1294 and added the outer walls. The place was never used in attack or defence so the decay began again and when the Bigods fell from power in 1306 the castle passed to Edward I.

A local roadbuilder bought it in 1766, planning to use the material for paving, but he broke every pickaxe in town before giving up. The castle remained. The next owner, Elizabeth Bonhote, built a cottage between the towers, but it was demolished in 1841. The castle now belongs to the town council and is locked, but you may borrow the keys from several shops in town. Access is therefore limited to shop opening hours.

Black Shuck. On 4 August 1577 Black Shuck, disguised as a thunderstorm, struck the town after hitting Blythburgh. But in 1688 the town suffered far worse when fire wiped out most of the timber-and-thatch houses. St Mary's Church was gutted and even the bells melted. The year after, the townspeople built the **Buttercross** to commemorate the fire, and nearby is an imprint of Black Shuck on a streetlamp.

South-west of the town is the **Flixton Aviation Museum** near the site of the wartime RAF Flixton. Open at limited times, the museum has a wide range of non-airworthy craft from the Spitfire to the Super Sabre. All came by road except the Vickers Valletta, which came slung under a helicopter.

THE OTTER TRUST
See page 88 for this intriguing attraction.

●

TOURIST OFFICES IN THE AREA
Aldeburgh The Cinema, High St, IP15 5AU, 01728.453637.
Beccles The Quay, Fen Lane, NR34 9BH, 01502.713196.
Felixstowe Leisure Centre, Undercliff Road West, IP11 8AB, 01394.276770.
Ipswich St Stephen's Church, St Stephen's Lane, IP1 1DP, 01473.258070.
Lowestoft East Point Pavilion, Royal Plain, NR33 0AP, 01502.523000.

KINGS and QUEENS of ENGLAND

from 1066 to 1901

1066–1087 **William I,** William the Conqueror, first of the Norman kings. At the end of his reign the Domesday Book is compiled, listing everything of value in the land.

1087–1100 **William II,** William Rufus.

1100–1135 **Henry I,** The Lion of Justice, younger brother of William II. Dies in Normandy.

1135–1154 **Stephen.**

1154–1189 **Henry II,** who rules most of the British Isles and half of France. Feudalism dies at the start of his reign.

1189–1199 **Richard I,** Richard the Lion-Heart or *Coeur de Lion,* goes on crusades and spends only months in England.

1199–1216 **John,** called 'Lackland' because he loses much of the French territory.

1216–1272 **Henry III,** crowned at the age of 10. In his reign Magna Carta becomes recognised as the law of the land.

1272–1307 **Edward I,** in whose reign wool becomes of major economic importance, particularly in East Anglia.

1307–1327 **Edward II,** elder son of Edward I. He is deposed in favour of his son and allegedly murdered with a red-hot poker in the anus.

1327–1377 **Edward III.** The French liaison is breaking down and in 1338 the Hundred Years War begins against France. The Black Death strikes in 1348. By 1375 England has lost all but a few towns in France.

1377–1399 **Richard II.** The first experiment with the poll tax results in the Peasants' Revolt of 1381.

1399–1413 **Henry IV,** with a weak claim to the throne, survives several battles but dies of an epileptic fit.

1413–1422 **Henry V,** who recovers some of the French provinces, dies from dysentery at Vincennes, aged 36.

1422–1461 **Henry VI** becomes king at the age of eight months. After Joan of Arc is burned at the stake the Earl of Suffolk proposes Henry marry Margaret of Anjou. In 1453 the king goes mad, shortly before the Wars of the Roses.

1461–1483 **Edward IV** succeeds from the deposed Henry while Lancaster and York continue to fight. Edward dies from pneumonia, aged 40.

1483 **Edward V** reigns from 9 April to 25 June but is victim of intrigue and dies, one of the 'princes in the Tower.'

1483–1485 **Richard III,** Edward's uncle, seizes the throne but dies at the Battle of Bosworth.

1485–1509 **Henry VII** brings in the Tudor dynasty and invades France yet again, while Columbus discovers America.

1509–1547 **Henry VIII,** the most outrageous king on the English throne, takes six wives. Because the Pope refuses to acknowledge divorce Henry breaks from the Catholic Church and Protestantism begins. Cardinal Wolsey of Ipswich is for a while the power behind the throne. Henry dies, aged 55, from problems with his leg.

1547–1553 **Edward VI,** Henry's only son becomes king. The peasants revolt again in Norfolk in 1549, and Edward dies of tuberculosis, aged 15.

1553 **Lady Jane Gray** is proclaimed queen on 6 July but loses her support on the 19th; she loses her head the next year.

1553–1558 **Mary I** becomes queen while staying at Framlingham Castle, Suffolk. She marries Philip of Spain who claims the English throne – unsuccessfully. Mary dies from flu.

1558–1603 **Elizabeth I,** Good Queen Bess, is probably England's most charismatic queen. In her reign Drake sails around the world and later defeats the Spanish Armada.

1603–1625 **James I,** who is James VI of Scotland, unites the two kingdoms. Guy Fawkes tries to blow up Parliament.

1625–1649 **Charles I.** Charles dismisses Parliament in 1629, but it grows strong and in 1642 the Civil War starts, Parliament versus the Crown. Charles is publicly beheaded at Whitehall and the Monarchy falls.

1649–1660 **The Commonwealth.** Oliver Cromwell becomes Lord Protector.

1660–1685 **Charles II,** son of the last king, regains the throne. The Plague strikes in 1665 and the Great Fire of London destroys the city in 1666. Charles dies of apoplexy, having secretly received the last rites of the Catholic Church.

1685–1689 **James II** encourages Catholicism but is overthrown by a Protestant revolution.

1689–1702 **William III and Mary II** are offered the throne, but a Protestant succession is demanded. Mary dies from smallpox in 1694 and William rules alone.

1702–1714 **Anne,** daughter of James II, satisfies the legal requirement and so reigns. The 1707 Act of Union legally binds England and Scotland.

1714–1727 **George I** ushers in the House of Hanover. Sir Robert Walpole creates the post of Prime Minister. George has a heart attack near Osnabrück, aged 67.

1727–1760 **George II.** Britain expands into North America and India.

1760–1820 **George III,** the longest-reigning king.

1820–1830 **George IV.** An unpopular monarch, George dies of liver failure after too much drinking.

1830–1837 **William IV** dies from the same cause, aged 71.

1837–1901 **Victoria,** grand-daughter of George III, is the longest-reigning monarch of all, coming to the throne aged 18.

And more royal signatures: Richard II (Le Roy R2); Henry IV (HR); Henry V (RH); James I; Charles I; Edward V (R. Edwardus Quintus).

INDEX

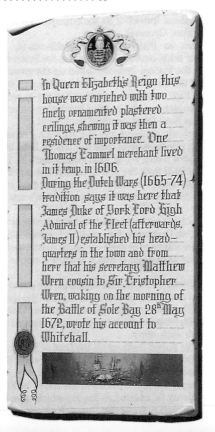

In Queen Elizabeth's Reign this house was enriched with two finely ornamented plastered ceilings, shewing it was then a residence of importance. One Thomas Cammel merchant lived in it temp. in 1606.

During the Dutch Wars (1665-74) tradition says it was here that James Duke of York Lord High Admiral of the Fleet (afterwards James II) established his headquarters in the town and from here that his secretary Matthew Wren cousin to Sir Cristopher Wren, waking on the morning of the Battle of Sole Bay 28th May 1672, wrote his account to Whitehall.